The Community of Swislocz, Grodno District
(Svislach, Belarus)

Translation of
Kehilat Svislots; Pelekh Grodno

Original Book Edited by: H. Rabin

Originally published in Tel Aviv by the former residents of Swislocz in Israel, 1961

JewishGen
מרכז עולמי לגנאלוגיה יהודית
The Global Home for Jewish Genealogy

A Publication of JewishGen
Edmond J. Safra Plaza, 36 Battery Place, New York, NY 10280
646.494.2972 | info@JewishGen.org | www.jewishgen.org

MUSEUM OF
JEWISH HERITAGE
A LIVING MEMORIAL
TO THE HOLOCAUST

The Community of Swislocz, Grodno District

Translation of *Kehilat Svislots; Pelekh Grodno*

Library of Congress Control Number (LCCN): 2024944544

ISBN: 978-1-962054-05-8 (hard cover: 182 pages, alk. paper)

About JewishGen.org

JewishGen, is a Genealogical Research Division of the Museum of Jewish Heritage - A Living Memorial to the Holocaust, serves as the global home for Jewish genealogy.

Featuring unparalleled access to 30+ million records, it offers unique search tools, along with opportunities for researchers to connect with others who share similar interests. Award winning resources such as the Family Finder, Discussion Groups, and ViewMate, are relied upon by thousands each day.

In addition, JewishGen's extensive informational, educational and historical offerings, such as the Jewish Communities Database, Yizkor Book translations, InfoFiles, Family Tree of the Jewish People, and KehilaLinks, provide critical insights, first-hand accounts, and context about Jewish communal and familial life throughout the world.

Offered as a free resource, JewishGen.org has facilitated thousands of family connections and success stories, and is currently engaged in an intensive expansion effort that will bring many more records, tools, and resources to its collections.

Please visit https://www.jewishgen.org/ to learn more.

Vice President for JewishGen: Avraham Groll

About the JewishGen Yizkor Book Project

Yizkor Books (Memorial Books) were traditionally written to memorialize the names of departed family and martyrs during holiday services in the synagogue (a practice that still exists in many synagogues today).

Over the centuries, as a result of countless persecutions and horrific atrocities committed against the Jews, Yizkor Books (Sefer Zikaron in Hebrew) were expanded to include more historical information, such as biographical sketches of famous personalities and descriptions of daily town life.

Following the Holocaust, the idea of remembrance and learning took on an urgent and crucial importance. Survivors of the Holocaust sought out other surviving residents of their former towns to memorialize and document the names and way of life of those who were ruthlessly murdered by the Nazis.

These remembrances were documented in Yizkor Books, hundreds of which were published in the first decades after the Holocaust.

Most of these books were published privately, or through *Landsmanshaftn* (social organizations comprised of members originating from the same European town or region) that still existed, and were often distributed free of charge. The languages used to document these crucial histories and links to our past were mostly Yiddish and Hebrew. JewishGen has undertaken the sacred responsibility of translating these books into English so that the culture and way of life of these communities will be preserved and transmitted to future generations.

In 1986, a group of farsighted JewishGenners started a project to pool their efforts together in groups based upon their ancestors' towns and donate funds to translate the Yizkor books of their ancestral towns into English. As the translated material became available, it was made accessible for free at https://www.JewishGen.org/Yizkor . Hardcover copies can be purchased by visiting https://www.jewishgen.org/Yizkor/ybip.html (see below).

It is our hope that the translation of these books into English (and other languages) will assist the countless Jewish family researchers who are so desperately seeking to forge a connection with their heritage.

Director of JewishGen Yizkor Book Project: Lance Ackerfeld

About JewishGen Press

JewishGen Press (formerly the Yizkor Books-in-Print Project) is the publishing division of JewishGen.org, and provides a venue for the publication of non-fiction books pertaining to Jewish genealogy, history, culture, and heritage.

In addition to the Yizkor Book category, publications in the Other Non-Fiction category include Shoah memoirs and research, genealogical research, collections of genealogical and historical materials, biographies, diaries and letters, studies of Jewish experience and cultural life in the past, academic theses, and other books of interest to the Jewish community.

Please visit https://www.jewishgen.org/Yizkor/ybip.html to learn more.

Director of JewishGen Press: Joel Alpert
Managing Editor - Jessica Feinstein
Publications Manager - Susan Rosin

Notes to the Reader

The images in the original book were reproduced from photographs from the time of the first edition. These reproductions were already of poor quality, being pre-war and at least 30 or more years old. As a result, the images in the book are the best achievable.

A reader can view the original scans of the book on the websites listed below.

The original book can be seen online at the Yiddish Book Center website:

https://www.yiddishbookcenter.org/collections/yizkor-books/yzk-nybc314033/rubin-hayim-1893-or-kehilat-svislots-pelekh-grodno

OR

at the New York Public Library Digital Collections website:

https://digitalcollections.nypl.org/items/9e39c890-3ae8-0133-3685-00505686a51c

To obtain a list of Shoah victims from **Swislocz, Belarus** the reader should access the Yad Vashem web site listed below; one can also search for specific family names using family name option. These lists are continually updated by Yad Vashem, so it is worthwhile to periodically search them.

There is more valuable information (including the Pages of Testimony, etc.) available on this website: https://yvng.yadvashem.org/

A list of all books available from JewishGen Press along with prices is available at: https://www.jewishgen.org/Yizkor/ybip.html

Additional resources for Swislocz are:

https://kehilalinks.jewishgen.org/Svisloch/

Cover Photo Credits

Cover Design by: Irv Osterer

Front Cover:
Design based on original cover (Adopted by Irv Osterer)

Back Cover:

Top Left: Hebrew Orphan Society [Page 72]

Top Right: Synagogue [Page 75]

Center: The Public Hebrew School in Svisloch [Page 46]
    Standing from right to left are the principals and teachers of the school:
    Reb Avraham Elkanitzki, Reb Chaim–Shlomo Shabzin, Yisrael Azerovitch,
    Naftali Eden, Yosef Katzenelboigen, Chaim Watnik, Kayla Eden, Alter
    Goldberg

Geopolitical Information

Map of Belarus showing the location of **Svislach**

Svislach Geopolitical Information

Svislach, Belarus is located at 53°02' N 24°06' E 155 miles WSW of Minsk

	Town	District	Province	Country
Before WWI (c. 1900):	Svisloch	Volkovysk	Grodno	Russian Empire
Between the wars (c. 1930):	Świsłocz	Wołkowysk	Białystok	Poland
After WWII (c. 1950):	Svisloch'			Soviet Union
Today (c. 2000):	Svislach			Belarus

Alternate Names for the Town:

Svislach [Bel], Svisloch' [Rus], Świsłocz [Pol], Sislevitsh [Yid], Svisločius [Lith], Śvisłač, Sislevitch, Sislevits, Svislovitch, Svislovitz, Svislotch, Svislots

Nearby Jewish Communities:

Golobudy 5 miles ESE
Jałówka, Poland 8 miles W
Mstibovo 8 miles NE
Vyalikaya Byerastavitsa 12 miles NNW
Porazava 13 miles ESE
Vawkavysk 17 miles ENE
Novy Dvor 17 miles SE
Gródek, Poland 19 miles WNW
Izabelin 19 miles ENE
Narewka, Poland 20 miles SW
Michałowo, Poland 21 miles W

Krynki, Poland 21 miles NW
Ros 21 miles NE
Lyskovo 25 miles ESE
Volpa 26 miles NNE
Narew, Poland 26 miles WSW
Białowieża, Poland 27 miles SSW
Odelsk 29 miles NNW
Kolonia Izaaka 29 miles NNW
Lunna 30 miles NNE
Hajnówka, Poland 30 miles SW
Indura 30 miles NNW

Jewish Population: 2,086 (in 1897), 1,959 (in 1921)

Introduction

Our goal was to make the English version of Kehilat Svislots come alive by translating it as literally as possible.

We wanted to ensure that the present and all future generations were able to hear the words in this book as they were spoken; to know the actual thoughts and words of those who remembered our families, and the place they called home.

The writers were not famous authors and wordsmiths skilled in the use of language.

Their concern was not the use of correct grammar, but rather, to preserve their memories of that time and that place.

You will certainly notice that, on occasion, certain ideas do not flow smoothly; there may be some incomplete thoughts, or some statements that just defy logic.

Certainly, there is a frustration that comes with everyone's desire for words to flow like novels on the Best Seller List.

But balance that desire with the magic of hearing the words as they were spoken to us; think of Tevia, in Fiddler on the Roof, and you can almost hear some of these words and phrases coming from his mouth.

A particular favorite of ours is the description of Aaron Isaac in the "Teachers of Sislevitch" article: "a tall man, with a nice built front and starched white cuffs, a bib, a starched collar with cuff links and a black top hat. His pride was in his brown mustache and pointy beard."

We can try to discern what the writer meant, that maybe he was handsome, muscular, fat, skinny, etc., etc.

But that would not be what was written, and in our opinion, it would be sacrilege to try and interpret these words.

Please note that all comments in parentheses are that of the translator.

Dedication

We humbly dedicate the translation of this book to the memory of all those who lost their lives through the senseless tragedy of the Holocaust. We particularly remember our family members, Kaplan, Vigonsky, Rosenbloom, Lappe, and Liss, and share the sadness of loss with all those whose family or families perished.

We also dedicate this to Mr. Joe Rozenberg, a 79 years old survivor of the Lodz Ghetto, who possesses a wonderful knowledge of Jewish history and customs and a man with a genuine understanding of English, Yiddish, German, and Polish.

Joe is a perfectionist and has donated hundreds of hours of time translating the Yiddish portion of the book, going over each article countless times to insure each one was as accurate and literal as possible.

We extend our heartfelt thanks to Joe for all his help.

Table of Contents

(Translator's Note: Chapters noted by (Y) are in Yiddish. All others are in Hebrew).

The Community of Swislocz, Grodno District (Svislach, Belarus)

53° 02' / 24° 06'

Translation of
Kehilat Svislots; Pelekh Grodno

Edited by: H. Rabin

Tel Aviv, former residents of Swislocz in Israel, 1961

Acknowledgments:

Project Coordinator

William K. Rosenbloom z"l

**Our sincere appreciation to Toby Bird z"l
for her excellent editing of the translated material**

**Our thanks to Sondra Ettlinger for extracting the pictures from the
original book,
enabling their addition to the project.**

This is a translation from: *Kehilat Svislots; Pelekh Grodno*
(The community of Swislocz, Grodno District)
ed. H. Rabin, Tel Aviv, former residents of Swislocz in Israel, 1961.

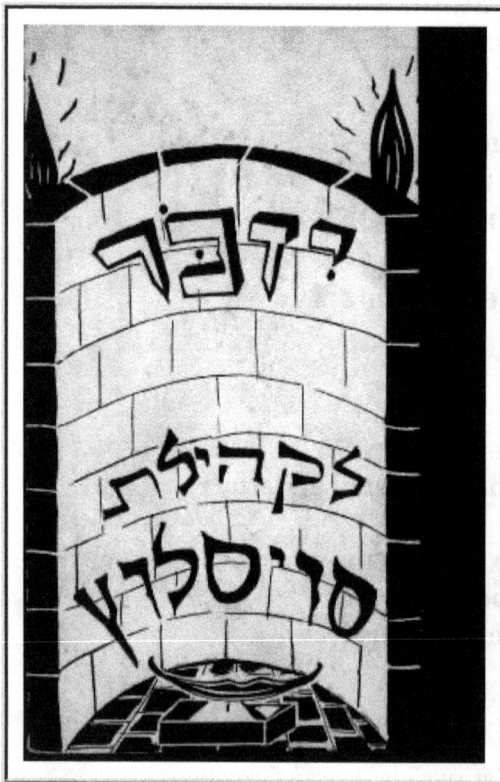

קהילת סביסלוץ

פלך גרודנא

העורך: ת. רובין

הוצאת עולי סביסלוץ בישראל
תשכ"א

[Pages 5-6]

Introduction

by the Editors

Translated by Jerrold Landau

One should not ask about the purpose of this book, just as one does not ask what moves a bereaved mother to mourn for her child. The bitterness of the bereavement and loss that fills the hearts of the survivors in every place demands salvation. In every memorial meeting for the martyrs, the request is made to perpetuate a dear town. Of all manners of perpetuation – monuments, institutions, etc. – the publication of a "Yizkor" book is considered to be the most appropriate. With the photographs of personalities, of institutions, or of various social groups, and through the various articles, one can feel the vibrancy and liveliness of the richness and poverty of those, who in the midst of their difficult battle for physical sustenance, dreamed of the revival of the nation, the language and the homeland, and yearned for personal redemption from slavery. Not only did they dream, but they also fought for actualization.

There is one additional aspect in all of these books.

The new generation in the Land[1] tends to look at the previous generations as lower in stature. It does not understand the splendor of the sublime might that exists in the struggle for existence in the Diaspora – and not merely physical existence. This generation sees hundreds of years of Jewish history as a thin page. This outlook is fatal to the Jewish imprint of the generation, for without these links, there is no historical foundation.

When these books will be found on the bookcases of thousands of families, they will look upon the rock that hewed them and stand on the strength and might, that despite the fact that they were a lamb among the wolves, created economic and spiritual creations, preserved their tradition, and served as the seed of the generation of independence.

We are sorry that this book is noted for its lacunae. It does not contain sufficient material to describe the personal and national vibrancy that percolated among the youth during those unsettled years. There were not enough preparations, and the lack of funds also constricted the material. Without any fault to us, the decision came to publish the book at a later time, and without any fault to us, a significant sum of money was collected and transmitted through the great toil of the activists in the United States.

The initiative of the book was taken by the natives of Svisloch in the Land, with great assistance from activists in the United States and Canada, and primarily with the assistance of the important activist who toiled without tiring for the benefit of our natives and for the perpetuation of the name of the town until the time of his death, Avraham Ayin of blessed memory.

Translator's Footnote:

1. In this translation, the term 'the Land' with a capitalized L, refers to the Land of Israel. It is a translation of the Hebrew word 'Haaretz'.

[Pages 7-8]

A view of the marketplace

The Community of Swislocz, Grodno District

Let us Remember[1]
A dirge

by Ch. Sh. Rubin (Egosewicz)

I will remember, I will remember you, the town of my birth;
Your well stocked market and its tied stalls,
Your outskirts, indeed two for the members of my nation;
With three – covered by the shadows of the tree,
Between the goaders of pigs and the cherry trees,
There were the stalls, do not be silent.

At this time and that time, your houses of worship
With the ringing of bells and the barking of dogs,
On the days of their festivals or in their festive processions,
Together in a large crowd, with crosses in their hands –
My eyes looked into their gaze as a serpent On the heights, I will divine your
enchantment.

I will remember, I will remember you on the autumn nights,
I stumble in your mud, in your wide marketplace
To the light of lanterns, with flashing shadows,
The deed of the children I the house. Greatly,
You pour your enchantment in the gold light.

During the blessed days, the fair took place in your midst,
With the shine of the foreheads of thousands of heads,
A Jew with a splendid beard stands out.
Lone among the many, outnumbered in the crowd,
He debates in Yiddish and the vernacular
Regarding a chicken and a hen
To raise them for Kapparot.

On the Sabbath eves, the sun
Is at its peak
Itzi Kaspar goes about
With his hoarse voice;
Householder, go to the bathhouse!
The marketplace is filled then like a fair,
Honorable people, the simple folk
The bath fees in their hand.

The day declines, before nightfall,
Shia the beadle, he elbows behind him,

He paces thunders with his thunderous voice;
To the synagogue the people should gather.

One after another, candles are lit,
The stars of below in the foggy light;
The ambience of holiness from the small sanctuaries
From one side to the other are enveloped with the crows of rest
With the chant of "The sanctuary of the king, the royal city"[2].

To the light of the burning candelabrum
On the holy Sabbath night
Between the courses, during the break
Father tests me in Chumash.

In my imagination, your sanctuaries now:
In a corner, in the dark –
The splendor of the graceful icon,

In a place, with bright letters
Of Mishnas and Gemaras,
In the closet over the chest of drawers,
Stare out and sight with the vision of generations.
Now in the yard, gnaw
The descendents of impure swine
Upon the pure holy pages.

You are fortunate, for I have been informed by those who came out of there
That you were burned completely at the stake
And the letters, like souls covered with blood
Ascended to on high with holiness and purity[3],
The toil and the seat of the wandering people
The enemy cannot destroy.

I remember you once more, with a curse on my lips.
Your rivers, your streams
Should turn to blood!
The should perish in you, you murderous city
All living things, all birds, all fish.

Because of the blood of my brothers and sisters
You have covered with your soil;
And with the gravestones of the graves of my ancestors
You have paved your sidewalks.

My brothers, my sisters in Sislovich
The tyrant did not leave a survivor from among you;
A mother and her children, with their death cries
They gave up their souls in the sludge of the Vishonik.
The orphan and the bereaved was its bitter lot
For those who remained in this world, will I remember.

The Vishonik Forest, woven with lights and shadows
In you I enjoyed myself during the days of summer, as a relief from
The stench of my cheder, revolted by its walls,
How you have now turned upon me as a cemetery
For fathers, mothers, with infants in their bosoms!
Tell me, my forest, with the whisper of the leaves,
About the agonizing tortures;
And together we will gloomily recite
Yitgadal Veyitkadash.

Yitgadal Veyitkadash
Over crushed skulls
And shredded bellies;
A scream and a lament
With "Shma Yisrael"
Kel Maleh Rachamim,
Who is like You among the G–ds![4]

Sons and daughters of my forlorn nation
Tears do not flow for nothing.
The cup of tears is filled
A spark roasted in the ashes of the martyrs,
A flame arises from the many fires
For their journey, and a thousand generations;
For the seed of the Satan will yet fail for the remnant,
Its arms will be defeated with the help of the Rock of Israel.

Translator's Footnotes:

1. Parts of this poetic dirge are rather cryptic in nature. My translation may not reflect the true meaning properly. Other parts flow more naturally.
2. A snippet from the Lecha Dodi prayer of Friday nights.
3. A reference to a story in the Talmud during which Rabbi Chananya ben Tradyon was covered with Torah scrolls and set on fire by the Roman executioners. During his agonies, his students asked him what he saw, and he said, "parchment burning, and letters ascending on high". I suspect that the phrase 'you are fortunate', which seems quite out of place here, refers to the fact that the Jewish people as a whole continues on even after the Holocaust.

4. References to various Jewish prayers. Yitgadal Veyitkadash is the opening phrase of the Kaddish prayer, recited during synagogue services by mourners. Kel Maleh Rachamim is the opening phrase of the prayer for the dead. Shma Yisrael is the doxology recited during the daily prayers, but is also recited by those near death.

[Pages 9-12]

Svisloch

(Its history from an economic perspective[1])

by Avraham Ayin
(Secretary of the assistance committee of Svisloch natives in New York)

Translated by Jerrold Landau

The town of Svisloch, which was called Sislovitz or Shislovitz by the Jews, already existed from the 15th century. It belonged to landowners (poretzes) with the name Fakusz. In the 17th century, the town passed over to landowners with the name Kriszpinow. In the 18th century, it became the property of the Tyskowicz counts. Count Wyncenti Tyskowicz made great efforts to enlarge and beautify the town. He constructed a square marketplace surrounded by houses. In the center of the marketplace, he built a square podium with a base of about 4 meters square and a height of about 15 meters. A large brass image was displayed on top of the platform, from which a meter long brass rod extended. In the town, it was said that the platform and its metallic point were intended to serve for protection from lightning and fires… Five main streets extended out from the marketplace: 2 to the east, and one to each of the other directions. At the entrances to the city at the edge of the streets, there were gates built of stone ("Brom")[2]. Heavy doors closed them during the nights. Between the gates, the town was surrounded by deep ditches, so that the entry would only be through the aforementioned gates. At night, when the gates were closed, entry to and exit from the city was prevented. To the east of the marketplace, between Amstiwowa and Rudbaka streets, there was a section in which stores were built from large stones. The count used to conduct fairs there twice a year. Each fair lasted for four weeks. People from all of Lithuania and central Poland would come to the fairs. The merchants would display their wares in the stores. Tyskowicz planted a civic garden, containing walking paths, to the west of the city. A gymnasium was built in the southwest of the city, which in later years became a teachers seminary, that graduated teachers for the primary schools throughout the region of Grodno. With the passage of time, a synagogue courtyard was built to the northwest. In the southeast, houses were built along narrow lanes called "Okepes" (excavations).

Several fires broke out in Svisloch. Thrice, a large portion of the city went up in flames: in the 1830s, in the 1880s, and in the summer of 1910. After the fires, the town was rebuilt anew, and its external appearance was improved by walls and fine houses.

The Jewish Settlement in Svisloch

We do not know exactly when the Jewish settlement in Svisloch arose. However, it is clear that there was a Jewish settlement for two hundred years. The cemetery of the town serves as proof to this. The gravestones whose inscriptions can still be read are from the 18th century. However, there are stones older than these, from which the inscriptions have been obliterated. Furthermore, at the entrance to the cemetery, this is a section where the gravestones are sunken into the earth, and it is difficult to know that people were buried there.

From the evidence in the cemeteries, it is possible to deduce that the Jewish community was small. It only began to grow in the 18<supth< sup=""> century, when the town passed over to the Tyskowicz counts. Wyncenti Tyszowicz built up the shops and conducted the fairs. These brought in merchants from afar, who turned into permanent residents. I see corroboration of this in the history of my Ayin family, whose roots were in Grodno, and settled in Svisloch during the 18th century. These were called "novikim", which means newcomers in Russian. The Jewish settlement grew to the extent that in the 1847 census, there were 997 Jews in the community of Svislovich. In the subsequent 50 years, the population was doubled. According to a government census in 1897, the Jewish population numbered 2086 souls[3]. The population grew despite the emigration to England, America and Argentina[4]. The development in the town of the Jewish community, as well as the Christian community, spurred on the economic development of the Jewish population.

The Economic Life of the Jews of Svisloch

During the early years of the community, the majority of the Jews of Svisloch worked in the lumber and grain trades, and were shopkeepers and craftsmen. Business blossomed when Tyskowicz conducted the fairs. Hotels, guesthouses and taverns were built. During the 1830s, when the stores were burnt, and there was nobody to rebuild them (the counts of the Tyszkowicz were intermixed with the Polish uprising, and fled abroad), the large fairs ceased, and many Jews were left with a dearth of livelihood. The Jews began to seek out new sources of livelihood. Some studied tanning. At first, they worked the hides of large animals. Later, they learned to work with finer hides. For this purpose, experts were brought in from Germany who taught them how to work all sorts of good hides. The pioneers of tanning were Pinchas Brzanki, Sender Mincz, Eliahu Rubin and his sons Itche Pinchas Levinsztyk. Tanning increased significantly. At the end of the 19th century, there were already approximately 10 tanning enterprises in the town, which employed several hundred workers.

The profits of the tanning workers were higher than that of the tradesmen. At times, they were three times as high. The town was in need of outside workers. These were brought in from the neighboring towns and villages. The high standard of living of the workers, and their purchasing power, raised the standard of living of the shopkeepers and the tradesmen. The following were numbered among the shopkeepers: Zdanowicz, Olinski and Liss. Their shops were general stores. In these stores, one could purchase anything from a shoelace to a nickel samovar, salted fish, fine sardines, galoshes, fine hats, sheets, etc.

In 1906, when the railway line between Siedlice and Blagaya was completed, and there was a railway station 2 kilometers from the town, the contact with the larger cities of Volkovisk, Bialystock, and even the capital Warsaw improved. New residents were attracted to the town and the population grew. There were already approximately 3,500 Jews in Svisloch before the First World War. During the First World War, refugees arrived from the town of Lapitch, Minsk region, and some of them remained as permanent residents of Svisloch.

The Economic Situation after the First World War

After the First World War, the tanning industry in Svisloch operated only on a small scale, for the principal market for processed hides, Russia, was closed to Svisloch. Therefore, many residents were left without livelihood. Emigration from Svisloch increased on account of the economic recession and Polish anti–Semitism. They immigrated to wherever they could: Argentina, North America, and when the quotas to America were filled, immigration to the Land of Israel began. Nevertheless, due to natural increase, the number of Jews in the town did not decrease. At the time of the Nazi conquest of the town, the population numbered approximately 3,500.

The emigrants from Svisloch during the final decades congregated primarily in the cities of Liverpool, New York and Montreal. Most of them adjusted well and took their places in manufacturing and various professions. They also became involved in communal work. In this realm, it is fitting to mention Rabbi Dr. Belkin and David Lewis. The former is the son of Shlomo Belkin, a Hebrew teacher in Svisloch, a writer in Hebrew newspapers, and an activist in the Zionist movement in the town. His son Dr. Samuel Belkin studied in yeshivas in Poland and America, and earned his doctorate. Now he is the president of the Rabbi Isaac Elchanan Yeshiva and School[5].

David Lewis is the son of Moshe Lewis (Moshe Losz or Moshele Chatzkel's). His father Moshe was an activist in the Bund movement in Svisloch, and was active in the social and cultural life of the town. His son David currently lives in Montreal, where he serves as the general secretary of the Jewish Workmen's Circle of Canada[6]. He is a lawyer by profession, but he dedicates his time and energy to the S. S. P. He is also known in Socialist circles in the United States, and among the leaders of the workers in England.[7]

Translator's Footnotes:

1. There is a footnote in the text which reads as follows (note, the footnote is not marked in the text itself – this is probably an omission): I extracted the historical facts from a research work that was written by Waclaw Kozlowski, a student of the teacher's seminary in Svisloch.
2. There is a footnote in the text here which reads as follows: In my day, there were no more than 3 "fromim": the other ones, on the roads from Brisk and Grodno, were no longer in existence at that time. (Translator's note, in the text, the term is "brom", whereas in the footnote it is "from" – singular of "fromim").
3. There is a footnote in the text here which reads as follows: The number of Jews in 1847 and 1897 were taken from a Jewish encyclopedia in Russian (Yevreyskaya Encyclopedia).
4. There is a footnote in the text which reads as follows: A number of Jewish families immigrated to Argentina in the 1890s, where they settled in the land of Moshavat Chevon.
5. I.e. Yeshiva University of New York.
6. David Lewis was later to become head of the New Democratic Party of Canada (i.e. the Socialist Party of Canada), and served as a prominent parliamentarian.
7. There is a footnote in the text which reads as follows (note, the footnote is not marked in the text itself – this is probably an omission): Regarding the Land of Israel, BL"S worked with a national feeling that was nurtured by Hebrew education and the political events that are described in other articles in this anthology (the translator and the editor).

[Pages 13-18]

History of the Community of Svisloch

by Reuven Egosewicz of blessed memory

Translated by Jerrold Landau

Reuven Egosewicz
of blessed memory

Reuven Egosewicz, the son of Reb Eliahu and Rachel Horodner, lived in Svisloch until after the First World War. He received his rabbinical ordination, and preached to a traditional, social movement. He immigrated to Antwerp, Belgium, and devoted his time to research. He immigrated to the United States around 1930, where he continued on his research, leading a life of asceticism, researching the Talmud and its commentators. He published three books of research in Yiddish, "The Old Greek Philosophy", "Principles", "Faith and Apostasy", "Explanations on Baba Kama".[1]. He also left manuscripts. He died in Israel at the beginning of the year 5772[2].

All my efforts to find the first source from which Svisloch sprung were for naught. The paths led me only to the date 5570 (1809–1810). That year, the book "Marot Hatzovaot" (Colored Mirrors) by Gaon Rabbi Moshe Zeev the son of

Eliezer, which contains the approbation of the rabbi and Gaon Rabbi Yechezkel "Katzenelfoign", the head of the rabbinical court of the community of Svisloch[3].

47 years later, in the year 5617 (1856–1857), the famous rabbi and Gaon Rabbi Meir Yonah Shatz of blessed memory served in Svisloch. He was the author of the books "Hashiloach" on the aggadaic material of the Tractate Brachot, "Pesach Leil Shimurim" on the Passover Haggadah, "Petach Dvir" on the Itur, and Har Hamoria" on the laws of sacrifices from Maimonides ." Aside from those books that he succeeded in publishing during his lifetime, the following remain in manuscript form ready for publication: A short commentary on the entire Jerusalem Talmud; a commentary on "Hilchot Gedolot" that he wrote when he was the rabbi and head of the rabbinical court of Brest Litovsk; the book "Mei Shiloach" that is novellae on the aggadaic material of the Order of Moed, other novellae on halachot from the entire Talmud, and questions, responsa, and notes that were written in the margins of the Talmud, the Rif, the Rosh and the Ran; and also novellae on the Zohar and emendations to the Zohar and Machazor Kol Bo[4].

Rabbi Meir Yonah died in the year 5651 or 5652 (1890–1892). He served in the rabbinate of Svisloch from the year 5617 (1856–1857) until his death, aside from a short break in the interim where he served as the rabbi and head of rabbinical court of Brest Litovsk. From this we learn about the importance of the community of Svisloch at that time, for there was a relationship regarding Torah leadership between it and Brest Litovsk, whose rabbinical seat was considered as the most important of the entire region. The following are words that emanated from the pen of Rabbi Meir Yonah himself regarding Svisloch in his introduction to "Petach Hadvir" that was published in the year 5634 (1873–1874):

"We ask about the welfare of the guests, that is the people of the holy community of Svisloch in the midst of whom I have resided from the year 5617 (1856–1857). They have borne all of my faults. They are an honorable community. There are also those who are great in Torah and the fear of Heaven, upholders of Torah. Their Beis Midrash contains a library filled with old and new books."

The Torah greats of the year 5634 (1873–1874) had all passed away before I could know them. I only know from hearsay about the scholarship of my grandfather Reb Chaim Shmuel (the father of my mother Rachel of blessed memory), about whose greatness and righteousness they would speak wonders. He had the merit that they would wait for him before the repetition of the Shmone Esrei in the old Beis Midrash, the place of worship of Rabbi Meir Yonah[5]. Similarly, I have heard about Reb Baruch Ayin, who later lived in Amdur, that he was one of the Torah greats during the life of Rabbi Meir Yonah – as is evidenced by his book "Dvar Mitzvah" on the topic of the enumeration of the 613 commandments, and a commentary on the words of Maimonides in the Book of Commandments and "Yad Sharashim Asher Hishrish" by Baruch the son of Rabbi Eliahu Ayin of Svisloch, Warsaw 5644 (1883–1884).

In order to be able to properly appreciate the genius of Rabbi Baruch, it is sufficient to note the following fact: When Svisloch went up in flames in the summer of the year 5670 (1909–1910), and the old Beis Midrash that contained a rich treasury of old and new books was also burned, Rabbi Baruch wished to make up the loss to some degree, and he donated more than 500 valuable books. My brother Reb Yehuda Leib of blessed memory (who died after these lines were written), a great scholar who was asked to classify the books, expressed his astonishment that all of the books were full with glosses by Rabbi Baruch, and these were only a portion of the books from his collection.

I also merited to know Reb Moshe Zalman Rubinstein of blessed memory. Apparently, he was also a Torah great of the year 5634 (1873–1874). About him as well, and his scholarship and righteousness, legends were told. Even though their origins cannot be corroborated, the stories testify to his greatness[6].

During his old age, Reb Moshe Zalman sat in the Beis Midrash of Amstiwowa Street. My rabbi and teacher Rabbi Moshe David of blessed memory, the main teacher of the town, who was expert in the early and latter commentators, was also part of that group.

Several people with rabbinical ordination worshipped in the new Beis Midrash: Reb David Meisel – who had a sharp mind and was the son–in–law of Reb Shmuel Malshinker, Reb Meir Leibush and Reb Avraham Olkanicki.

It is fitting to devote a few lines to Reb Shmuel Malshinker himself. He was a Jew graced with fine traits, who devoted his energies to the Beis Midrash that was called by his name. He was a Torah reader, a prayer reader, and the teacher of Mishnah to the congregation. He set up the Beis Midrash as a study hall for Yeshiva students from out of town.

Reb Shlomo Belkin, also studied in the Beis Midrash of Reb Meir. He was known as a scholar in the Holy Language. He was a teacher. He was the father of Rabbi Dr. Samuel Belkin, the president of Yeshiva University. Reb Shmuel moved to Slonim when he was already in his forties, and received his rabbinical ordination.

However, the largest number of scholars was found in the old Beis Midrash. Reb Mordechai Slutski worshipped there. He was a scholar and a scribe, who himself authored books and edited the books of others[7]. Like him, Reb Yisrael Zelcer was a shamash in the Beis Midrash. The diligent studier Reb Leib Chaike's studied in this Beis Midrash. Reb Yosha Darciner, whose entire aspiration was to go to the Land, also worshiped there. Even the rabbi of the city Rabbi Yosef Rosen, who was later appointed as a rabbi in Passaic, New Jersey (U. S. A.) would pay attention to what he said.

Reb Yerachmiel would sit among the great scholars at the second part of the eastern wall. My father of blessed memory sat next to him. I permit myself to relate the following fact about my father: when I was in Bialystock, I entered the Beis Midrash to display my didactic powers that I had recently acquired from the Yeshiva of Mir. One of the scholars, who knew that I was from Svisloch, asked me who I was. When I told him that I was the son of Eliahu Horodner, he said to me, "Would it be that in another ten years, you would be known as your father."

The town did not only excel in scholarship. It excelled in dedication and activism without the expectation of obtaining a reward. When the Beis Midrash was burned among other buildings, Reb Shmuel Malshinker volunteered for the manual labor. He worked with mortar and bricks, and simultaneously did not neglect his communal work. All of this was not for personal benefit. In this manner, Reb Shmuel was not exceptional. Reb Yosef Katzenelboigen (Yoske Grodzinkes, a descendent of the famous Rabbi of Brisk Rabbi Avraham Katzenelboigen) dedicated his entire life to communal work: the Talmud Torah and Zionism. He was also selected to one of the first Zionist congresses. An important communal task was the responsibility of my father of blessed memory, who worked hard to support his household. He was the gabbai (trustee) of the old Beis Midrash, Maos Chittin (Passover charity) and Tzedaka Gedola. (My father of blessed memory was modest and did not belong to the wealthy class. From the 5–6 rubles that he earned a week, he was like Hillel in his time, dedicating half of it to tuition. Why did they see fitting, indeed, to give him the responsibility of such an important trusteeship?) My father's student in communal work, Reb Feivel Lev (Feivel the Goralnik) later accepted communal work upon himself. We should mention Reb Melech "the Valker" – a righteous man who performed the most difficult and menial charitable acts. He would visit the sick and tend to them even during an epidemic. He would comfort the bitter of heart. If Reb Melech saw a Jew working hard, he would immediately help him in order to fulfill the commandment "You shall surely bear his burden with him".

Here is not the place to describe our town, particularly because my friend Avraham Ayin already preceded me[8]. I wish only to mention people whom I was together with, or who I knew them in some capacity; these proved that the town in its youth did not embarrass its elders. I knew the friend of my elder brother Chaim Shmuel Aharon the son of the rabbi (the son of the rabbi of the city, the rabbi and Gaon Shneur Zalman Pines of blessed memory) who was later known in the Slobodka Yeshiva as "the Genius from Svisloch", and of whom great things were told about him as well in other Yeshivas. Today he is known as the splendid Gaon Rabbi Aharon Kotler.

Another friend of my brother was the rabbi and Gaon Rabbi Feivel Rubin of blessed memory who became known as a Torah great in Lida and Ponovitch. The conditions of his life brought him to a situation where he began to work in the tannery of his grandfather, to the perspective of "a plate of platon[9] placed in a dirty place". He met his death at the hands of the Nazis. I also wish to mention my friend who succeeded in Torah, the head of the Yeshiva of Volozhin, the rabbi and Gaon Rabbi Shimon Langbard, who lives in the Land of Israel.

Many scholars and maskilim were natives of this town. Some of them passed away and some are alive. Some are scribes and disseminators of Torah, and others are active in communal life. These are only a small part of the intellectual fruit that the town of Svisloch produced. These are the ones I knew. Some of them were known as Svislochites because they remained in the town for only a short time[10].

Considering that the town of Svisloch is only a tiny point on the map of cities and towns in which the Nazi monster wreaked destruction, it can be seen from here the type of fruitful garden of intellect that the Nazi beast cut off with its destruction.

Translator's Footnotes:

1. Four are listed here, although the number given in the text is three. Baba Kama is a Talmudic tractate.
2. It is currently the year 5766 (2005–2006), so this date is obviously in error.
3. There is a long footnote in the text as follows: Note: it is appropriate to point out that Reb Yechezkel of blessed memory was the third child of the famous rabbi of Brisk, Rabbi Avraham Katzenelboigen of blessed memory, the father of seven sons (see page 17 in Daat Kedoshim of Eisenstadt Viener). From that research, it can be deduced that Rabbi Yechezkel was already elderly in 5570 (1809–1810). In that research, it appears that Rabbi Yechezkel did not occupy any rabbinical post prior to Svisloch. From there, it appears that he served for many years in Svisloch prior to the aforementioned date, since, as was usual, first rabbinical posts were taken by rabbis in their younger days. It appears that Rabbi Yechezkel was greatly honored among Torah scholars. As proof to this, the aforementioned Rabbi Moshe Zeev, who was so great in Torah that he was appointed as the head of the rabbinical court of Bialystock, sought after the approbation of Rabbi Yechezkel for his book after he already had obtained the approbation of the rabbi of Brisk. From this we learn that Svisloch was a very important community.
4. There is a footnote in the text as follows: See "A Bitter Eulogy on Rabbi Shmuel Mohilever" written by the son of Rabbi Meir Yonah, the rabbi and Gaon Reb Mordechai, who was also a rabbi in Svisloch.
5. There is a footnote in the text that reads as follows: I heard this from the mouth of Reb David Brzkowski, one of the elders of Svisloch, who serves as the shamash in the Beit Yisrael synagogue in New York. One can rely on his words, for he was already an adult at the time, and from the death of Grandfather until the present sixty hears have not passed, and it says "one remembers until sixty years". I was fortunate to know this Reb David well, for through him, one can peer at the G–d fearing characters that Reb Meir Yonah mentions. This Reb David upholds the adage "The moon was not created except for learning", for he sits until after midnight during the night

studying Mishnah. However, he does not act haughtily as a scholar, for according to the Halacha he is forbidden to fast. He also fasts on BaHab, on the eve of Rosh Chodesh (Yom Kippur Katan) and on Mondays and Thursdays – of which I am familiar from my youth. (Translator's notes: the latter listed fast days are minor fast days observed by custom by especially pious people. The last sentence is somewhat garbled, and does not seem to make sense.)

6. There is a footnote in the text as follows: In New York, his granddaughter married Mr. Avraham Ayin, the secretary of the Svisloch Mutual Benefit Organization. Mr. Avraham Ayin was a relative of Rabbi Baruch. Reb Zeev Ayin of blessed memory also belonged to this family. His elder brother Reb Moshe Ayin gave over to me the genealogy of his relative Reb Baruch Ayin.

7. There is a footnote in the text as follows: The book of Rabbi Mordechai Slutski was entered into the catalog of the Jewish Theological Seminary under the name of "Azharot for the Festival of Shavuot" by Rabbi Eliahu the Elder, with the commentary from the old generation, published anew and with a commentary called Hidur Zaken, Mordechai Slutski of Svisloch, Warsaw, 5660 (1899 – 1900).

8. There is a long footnote in the text as follows: See the article of Avraham Ayin "The Town of Sislovich" in "YIVO pages", September–October 1944. Similarly, "The Economic Life of Sislovich", May–June 1945. I pointed out to Mr. Ayin several lacunae in his article, which he himself expressed his wish that I fill. For example, in his description of a wedding in Sislovich, he neglected to mention the feast for the poor that was no less fancy than the feast for the relatives and friends, and at times even more so fancy. One must not forget that this feast was not to find favor in their eyes, but exactly the opposite, to find favor solely in G–d's eyes. Poor people from the area would gather together for this feast. Among them were talented jesters and good hearted beggars who entertained the guests. Other ceremonial meals such as the feast of the "Chevra Lina" would instill light in the darkness of the life of the exile. The charitable distributors of Maos Chittin and Tzedaka Gedola, as well as the providing for guests that Father of blessed memory busied himself with along with Reb Zelig of blessed memory (The Oleboder teacher) the trustee of Hachasat Orchim – would relate to the recipients in an honorable manner, in particular to the poor who would receive charity from Tzedaka Gedola. The recipient would feel no lack of his honor.

9. I am not sure what the word 'platon' is referring to here. It could mean one of: Plato, feuilliton, or platinum. The adage is unclear.

10. As an example, I mention the name of Mr. David Lewis (Losz), a famous lawyer and the national secretary of the Canadian Socialist union.

[Page 19]

The Spiritual Leaders

by the Editor

Translated by Jerrold Landau

As in other Jewish communities, the spiritual leadership was in the hands of the rabbis. Differentiating between kosher and treif (non–kosher), family life (marriage and divorces), Torah based court cases between man and his fellowman, representation before the government, primary supervision over the houses of prayer and charitable institutions – all of these were decided by the rabbi. It goes without saying that all of these demanded an understanding of life, practicality, personalities, and the power of convincing. However, in a place where in the eastern wall of the synagogue, all of the laymen who were great in Torah were sitting, it was up to the rabbi to supercede them all in Torah so that they would relate to him with honor. Thus was it in Svisloch two generations ago, when the Beis Midrashes were rich with laymen who were great scholars, and they determined who was fitting to serve as the rabbi of the town. Greatness in Torah was what made a rabbi fitting for his position. The rest of the requirements were of secondary importance. When the scholars of the town became fewer, the weight of other characteristics, such as impressive appearance, wisdom of life, oratory skill, etc. grew in importance.

As we have read in the previous article, we have no information regarding spiritual life of the town from the early generations. Only little is known about Rabbi Yechezkel Katzenfoigen and later about the Kochav Hameir Rabbi Meir Yonah.

The History and Personality of Rabbi Meir Yonah the Commentator on Haiatur

by the Editor

(From what was told to his grandson the writer Yaakov Rabinowitz to Dr. B. M. Lewin)

Translated by Jerrold Landau

Rabbi Meir Yonah (his family name was Brancki, and in order to clear up some confusion, in his old age he received a passport with the name Meir Yonah Glanowski) was born in the year 5577 (1716–1717) to his father Rabbi Shmuel Zalman who was the rabbi of Suchowola near Bialystock.

After his father died in the prime of his life, Rabbi Meir occupied the rabbinical seat of Suchowola at the age of 18. From there he moved to Porozowa, where his father had served as a preacher and judge before he moved to the rabbinate of Suchowola. From there he moved to Konyuszany and from there to Svisloch (called Shishlovitz, in the Horodno region). In the year 5632 (1871–1872) he was accepted as the rabbi and head of the rabbinical court of Brest Litovsk (Brisk) (see Ir Tehila, the book on the community of Brisk and its rabbis). After he lived in Brisk for a year and a half without his family (his wife was a merchant and did not want to leave her store and be dependent on the rabbinical salary, he was forced to return to Svisloch. Brisk took Rabbi Yosef Ber[1], the father of Rabbi Chaim Brisker, as a rabbi. Rabbi Meir Yonah dedicated his efforts to books that were thought of as stepchildren, and that were not dealt with much or even only very little (The Jerusalem Talmud, the Itur, Halachot Gedolot, and the orders on the Temple service and sacrifices by Maimonides). In the year 5634 (1873–1874), he published the second volume of the Itur, a book that had been dealt with in the ancient tradition (see Shem Gedolim and Orchei Haitur by Rabbi Yerucham). Heavy tragedies in his family had an ill effect on him, however he overcame them and completed the first half of the first section in 5643 (1882–1883), and the second half in 5648 (1887–1888) (see the end of his introduction to the second half of the first section of the Itur).

The Gaon Rabbi Meir Yonah

The publisher Reb Yitzchak Goldman advised Rabbi Meir Yonah to emend the text of the Itur internally with his glosses and notes; and if he wishes to maintain the unclear versions, he should only include them in his notes. If he were to do this, Reb Yitzchak would take it upon himself to publish it, and would also provide him with funds, books and the like to ease his work on his other books. However Rabbi Meir Yonah trembled and said, "Far be it from me to touch the ancient text, even if it is unclear. All emendations are only speculation, and if I were to err, Heaven forbid, I would mislead the public."

In the years 5643–5644 (1882–1884), he also published his book on the Passover Haggadah called Lepesach Leil Shimurim, and his book Mei Shiloach on the legends of tractate Berachot of the Talmud.

In the year 5647 or 5648 (1886–1888), the first section of his great work on the section of his large book on the sections of the Temple service and sacrifices of Maimonides was published.

Rabbi Meir Yonah's energy for work was boundless. Until he took ill, he was particular about his daily hour–long walk outside the city, even on rainy and snowy days. He became ill with cancer in the year 5650 (1889–1890) and died on the 17th of Sivan 5651 / June 23, 1891).

The following manuscripts remain from him: four large volumes on the Jerusalem Talmud (in which he also included the novellae of his eldest son Rabbi Avraham Aharon, who began to write a commentary on the Jerusalem Talmud, but only succeeded in completing the order of Zeraim[2], for he died at the age of 49). In the year 5644 (1883–1884), he completed two large volumes of Hilchot

Gedolot, Mei Shiloach on the legends of the Order of Moed, and a book on Maimonides. All of these were burned along with his entire library in the large fire that took place in Svisloch a few years before the war.

Rabbi Meir Yonah was an Orthodox man, and very particular to the point of extremism. During his youth, he would persecute Hassidim. He aroused the wrath of the wealthy and well placed people of his city when he took the side of the laborers and the poor. In his last years, he was also persecuted by them. He never extended a greeting to any person who came to him as long as he thought that he was coming for a Torah judgment. He would not look at the disputants until he had issued a legal decision. After that, he would ask them to sit down, and would greet nicely any guest who came to his door.

He preferred breadth to depth in his style of learning. In his library, there was almost no book without his notes on the margins, including in the Zohar and the prayer book of the Ari (Rabbi Yitzchak Luria).

His hatred of Hassidism (that weakened in his latter years of life, when he would even speak in their praise, after the denigration of religion increased in his place) did not interfere with him occupying himself with books of the hidden Torah[3], even though he discouraged others from occupying themselves with them.

In laws of the permitted and forbidden, civil laws, he would deal primarily with the early rabbis. (An adage said in his name was, "I myself am a latter rabbi".)

I heard the following story from the butchers of a city near Svisloch. Once on the night before Passover, he sat for eight hours until the morning, searching for a possibility of declaring kosher an ox that had cost the butchers 80 rubles, and if it were to be declared non–kosher, the city would be left without meat for Passover. In the morning, he sent his shamash (assistant) to call together a quorum of laymen. Together with them, and under the responsibility of all of them, he declared the ox to be kosher. When one of the laymen challenged him, he stamped upon him with his foot. The butchers said that in his day, they became rich, and after his death, they became poor. Despite this, he was strict upon himself.

The gentiles of the region who would come before him for judgments with Jews, would place oil into the eternal lamp on his grave after his death (something that became evident after beadle had forgotten a few times to put oil in the lamp during days of snow and mud, and it was found burning. After the matter was investigated, it was discovered that gentiles had put oil in it.)

From among his children, it is worthwhile to note the following: a) Rabbi Avraham Aharon (family name is Rabinowitz), a great expert in the Jerusalem

Talmud and early rabbis, a very modest man, and a bit of a Maskil, who was accepted as a rabbi in Konyuszany, and left the rabbinate in the middle of the night out of fear because of the shadows of a dispute; b) Rabbi Mordechai (family name is Shatz), a man of generous character traits, a modest man who forewent his own honor, who had a bitter spirit in his old age after he had lived a bitter life because of the dispute in Svisloch. He was the rabbi of the minority in a city where the majority, including the wealthy of the city, took for themselves a different rabbi. This Rabbi Mordechai was among the first in Bialystock of those who purchased land in Petach Tikva.

(Note: from among the grandchildren of Rabbi Meir Yonah, it is worthwhile to note the famous writer Yaakov Rabinowitz, who died in the Land; and, may he live, Mr. Avraham Glin, a Maskil, the author of the book Ayin Beayin, and among the first settlers of Ein Ganim in Petach Tikva.)

Translator's Footnotes:

1. Soloveitchik
2. The first of the six orders of the Mishna.
3. Hassidism places a stress on the hidden (i.e. mystical) aspects of the Torah.

[Page 22]

The Rabbis after Rabbi Meir Yonah

Translated by Jerrold Landau

**Rabbi Mordechai
the son of Rabbi Meir Yonah**

Rabbi Mordechai the son of Rabbi Meir Yonah Shatz

He was known just as Rabbi Mordechai, without the title of Rabbi of the City. He had an impressive appearance, was modest, and avoided disputes even though disputes followed him. After the passing of Rabbi Meir Yonah, his son was not invited to serve in his place. In the city, they would say that this was because Rabbi Meir Yonah did not command that his son should be the rabbi of the city, certainly because he did not feel him worthy of such. I heard from Mr. Avraham Glin the grandson of Rabbi Meir Yonah that at first Rabbi Mordechai was wealthy. He was a large–scale merchant of dyes in Bialystock who also had business connections with London. However, he suffered great losses during a recession. He sold everything in order to pay his debts, including the plot of land that he had purchased in Peach Tikva. After he lost his fortune, he answered the call of some of the residents of the city to serve as rabbi, even though most of the residents of the city had accepted Rabbi Shneur Zalman Pines as rabbi, who was known by the name of "Stadtrav". Rabbi Mordechai was loved by the masses on account of modesty. Even though members of his community were very dedicated to him, he lived a life of poverty and tribulation. He had a minyan in his home, and only on festivals would he would he come to the synagogue where the simple masses would congregate, for the honorable and wealthy people of the community would be in the Beis Midrash. Rabbi Mordechai wrote several books: Ahavat Mordechai, Torat Mordechai, and Hesped Mar (Bitter Lamentation, about Rabbi Shmuel Mohilever, the rabbi of Bialystock and one of the first of Chovevei Tzion).

Recorded from the mouth of Mr. A. Glin

[Page 23]

Rabbi Shneur Zalman Pines of blessed memory[a]

He was accepted as rabbi by most of the town, including the scholars. He was short, thin, and weak, and despite all of this he was accepted as the rabbi after Rabbi Meir Yonah of blessed memory for no other reason than his greatness in Torah. I remember him from my childhood. I would visit the house of the rabbi as a friend of the delightful child Arka (today the Rabbi and Gaon Rabbi Aharon Kotler). We studied together with Father of blessed memory, and we sat on "watch"[2] together. The house of the rabbi shone with the splendor of the Gaon. Wonders were spoken about the eldest daughter. She excelled with her sharp intelligence, and knowledge of Hebrew and the sciences. Later, she became a doctor. Arka was extolled for his sharp answers to the questions of the teachers.

The rabbi himself spoke very little. His voice was weak, his words were pleasant, and he was greatly honored by the important people of the city. On festivals, he would preach primarily about matters of Halacha and would receive signs of approval from the scholars.

The dispute between the sides was conducted with bitterness, but his voice was not heard. Nevertheless, apparently this dispute was one of the factors that led to his untimely passing.

The Editor

Original footnote:

1. I approached the son of the Rabbi and Gaon Aharon Kotler[1] several times in order to receive information on the story of his life, but to my dismay, I was not answered. I was forced, therefore, to write something from my memory. The editor.

Translator's Footnotes:

1. He was the Rosh Yeshiva of the very large Lakewood Yeshiva of New Jersey.
2. Mishmar or "watch" is an all night learning session.

[Page 24]

Rabbi Yosef Rozen of blessed memory

Rabbi Yosef Rozen and his wife

After the death of Rabbi Shneur Zalman, Rabbi Yosef Rozen was accepted as the rabbi of Svisloch. He had an impressive appearance, thin, tall, with a countenance that exuded good naturedness. His scholarship exuded sharpness. In addition, he was intelligent and expert in the matters of the world. Therefore, even people who tended toward skepticism would come to him for Torah judgments. He would always lean toward the path of compromise. In a dispute, he would mediate between the disputants, to their mutual satisfaction.

He did not particularly excel as a preacher, and he did not have the power to move hearts. However, he words were filled with content and sharpness. The scholars – and there were many scholars in Svisloch – were particularly satisfied.

He was not extremist in his Orthodoxy, and he was able to accommodate the spirit of the times.

Most of the people of the community were on his side. As previously, a few stood at the side of Rabbi Mordechai Shatz, who cloistered himself within the four ells of Halacha and did not become involved in the dispute that became sharper and more serious even with the success of Rabbi Rozen. My father of blessed memory said that the rabbi complained before him and expressed his bitterness about the dispute, to the point where he loathed the rabbinical seat of the town. After the First World War, he moved to America, and obtained an honorable position in Passaic near New York.

He was tied to the Land of Israel with the strands of his soul, and he even invested money there. He purchased property in Jerusalem, and visited Israel at set times. He died at an old age.

Y. D. Egosewicz

[Page 25]

The Rabbi and Gaon Rabbi Mordechai Dov Eidelberg,may G–d avenge his blood

**Rabbi Mordechai Dov Eidelberg,
may G–d avenge his soul**

He was born in the year 5640 (1879–1880) to his father the rabbi and Gaon Rabbi Yitzchak of blessed memory, a rabbi in the region of Bialystock, a descendent of Rabbi Tzvi Hirsch Friluker, and adherent of Brisk, a descendent of the Rema of blessed memory.

Rabbi Mordechai Dov was numbered among the expert students of the Chofetz Chaim of holy blessed memory, whose Torah and ways were his path of life. He authored books on Halacha (law) and Aggada (lore). As is related, the Chofetz Chaim of holy blessed memory set aside times to study his compositions.

He married his life's partner, the righteous, pure of heart and pure of deed, Mrs. Chaya Applebaum, who came from a family of Torah greats. She was the granddaughter of the author of Kerem Chemed on the four sections of the Code of Jewish Law, and a descendent of other such individuals.

After his marriage, he studied in Volozhin, and was known there as the Diligent One of Bialystock. He received his rabbinic ordination from the leaders of the generation, including the Gaon Rabbi Rafael Shapiro of holy blessed memory, who honored him to the degree that when he was to be out of town, he delegated legal decisions on the permitted and forbidden to this Rabbi Mordechai.

He served as a Rabbi in Liska, Lithuania, and in Kantakuzovka of the region of Charzon, where he wrote his halachic work Dovev Siftei Yeshanim in memory of his mother, peace be upon her. This book was burnt in the fire that broke out in the publishing house of Poltava.

In the year 5677 (1916–1917), he was accepted as the rabbi in the city of Nikolaev of the region of Charzon. He managed to bring many closer to Judaism due to his fiery speeches, primarily the youth who had turned to the Left leaning parties in that era. With the outbreak of the war, pogroms broke out in the city and the region, and Jews were killed on the roads and attacked in the cities by bands of murderers. Many refugees from the region streamed to Nikolaev, and the rabbi knew how to protect them within the community due to his connections with the government. When the Red Army captured Nikolaev, they imprisoned the leaders of the city, including the rabbi. He was freed after a short time, and the government issued an apology for his imprisonment.

During these difficult years, his house was open to any in need, any who were hungry or thirsty. Once during the years of famine, it happened that one of those who came snatched a half a loaf of bread from the table of his house. This loaf was obtained after standing in line for many hours. When the members of the household suggested to the rabbi that he should close the door so that the house will not be a free–for–all for everybody, he did not agree, saying: "All those in need are like children to the rabbi, and one does not close the door before children.

In the year 5682 (1921–1922), when the refugees were permitted to return to Poland from Russia, the rabbi of Bialystock returned to his native city. There, he did a great deal to help the rabbis who had suffered in Russia, via an organization that sent food packages there. There, he also published the first section of his book Chazon Lamoed, a book of responsa and investigation on realistic topics of the time in Soviet Russia.

In the year 5684 (1923–1924) he was appointed as the rabbi of Svisloch, Grodno region, a relatively well–off town. This community regarded its rabbi with honor and esteem. Through his sermons, he worked for the strengthening and the study of Torah. Their reverence for their rabbi extended to the point that the entire community accompanied him when he took leave of them.

From Svisloch, he moved to Makow in central Poland. He endeared himself greatly to the people of the community, despite the fact that the city was hassidic and he was a Misnaged. This was because of his greatness in Torah, his generous character traits, and his honesty. He always stood by the working people. Even the head of the Bund chapter would bring labor disputes between the workers to the rabbi.

In the year 5688 (1927–1928), he was chosen as the rabbi of Plock on the Wisla River. There too, all streams of the community loved him, including the assimilationists. Benevolent organizations were founded in city thanks to his efforts. In Plock, he published three move volumes of his work Chazon Lamoed. The fourth volume was dedicated to the laws of the second day of festivals in the Diaspora.

His activities also spread out beyond the borders of Plock. He was a member of the active committee of the Union of Rabbis of Poland. He assisted the Yeshivas of Lithuania, and he appeared before the government and the ministries of Poland. He was invited to adjudicate complex cases that even involved gentiles, and they placed their trust in him.

The relationship of the rabbi to the Land of Israel was one of love and dedication. He sent three of his sons to the Land of Israel to study Torah.

In the year 5690 (1929–1930), he visited the Land for the marriage of his son. Rabbi Kook of holy blessed memory wished to appoint him as the rabbi of Petach Tikva. However because of the many urgings of the people of Plock, he pushed off his settlement in the Land for some time. In the interim, he purchased a plot of land around Gan Yavneh. However, he stumbled upon untrustworthy people, and he lost his money without receiving the Land.

During the time of the Holocaust, when the Germans entered Plock, they tortured the rabbi and made him perform hard labor.

He fled from Plock to Lomza, and was accepted as a rabbi there. From there, he wandered about and arrived in Lachowka, where he was accepted as a rabbi. There, he concerned himself with providing assistance to the rabbis in exile in Siberia. His letters attest to the greatness of his spirit, and to the help that he extended to his fellow during those difficult days.

In one of his letters, he writes about his invitation to serve as a rabbi in the community of Novorodok.

"I am disinclined from accepting this position because I have enough for me and for the sustenance of my grandson Yitzchak Nechemia[1] may G–d avenge his blood (the son of his daughter Reizl and son–in–law the rabbi and Gaon Rabbi Chaim Goldstein, who accompanied him on his wanderings), and also to send a package to the family in Plock. Here in Lachowka, I have the peace to be able to dedicate myself diligently to Torah, and to arrange my writings."

On the 8th of Cheshvan 5702 (1941), the bitter and violent day, the rabbi sanctified the Name of his Creator along with hundreds of Jews of Lachowice may G–d avenge their blood, who were taken to be murdered by the Germans, may their names be blotted out.

May his holy and pure soul be bound in the bonds of life along with all of the martyrs of the Holocaust.

Written by his son in the Land of Israel

Translator's Footnote:

1. "May G–d avenge his blood" appears after the name – but it would appear that at the time, the grandson was alive. This sentence seems to intermix the first person and third person in the narrative.

[Page 28]

Rabbi Chaim Yaakov Miszkinski of blessed memory, the Last Rabbi of Svisloch

Rabbi Chaim Yaakov Miszkinski, a noble and unusual personality, was born in 5643 (1882–1883) to his father Rabbi Moshe Yehuda, a tenant on an estate in Berezniki, Suwalki region. He studied Torah from the mouths of the greats in the Yeshivas of Radin, Knesset Yisrael in Slobodka, and the Kolel in Volozhin. In Slobodka, he became attached to the Mussar (morality) method of Rabbi Yisrael Salanter. The portent of his life was Rabbi Yitzchak Blazer (Reb Itzele Peterburger) who was revered by him so much that he called his eldest son Yitzchak.

Chaim Yaakov Miszkinski
may G–d avenge his blood

The Mussar methodology forged his character. He had generous character traits that were expressed already in the Yeshivas. Since he was the son of wealthy parents, his friends in Yeshiva would borrow from him and return the money to him after many years. He helped them not only monetarily but also bodily: he took care of his sick friends, even if the illness was contagious. He married the daughter of the rabbi of Konyuszany Rabbi David Pines. He first served as the rabbi of Stobno, Suwalki region. This town was destroyed during the First World War. The family of the rabbi also suffered from wanderings and losses. When Rabbi David Pines was called to serve in the rabbinate of Bialystock, his son–in–law Rabbi Chaim Yaakov filled his position in Konyuszany. He was loved by the members of the community, who recognized him as a true judge and as someone who was concerned about anyone who was suffering from a difficult lot. There were many stories about his righteousness.

During the time of the German occupation during the First World War, he did a great deal to lighten the suffering of his townsfolk that was caused by the tyranny of the rulers. When someone from the town was arrested on account of smuggling, the rabbi interceded on humanitarian grounds to ensure that all of the merchandise would not be confiscated, so that the staff of bread would not be cut off from the families. He did not cow before threats of imprisonment, and he succeeded in assuaging the anger of the ruler and in swaying him to his will. With his impressive appearance, the pleasantness of his ways, and his knowledge of foreign languages, he won the hearts of the rulers. The ruler of the town became a friend of the rabbi, and wished to improve his status. Once he advised him to accept a milk–cow, a source of salvation in those days. However, the rabbi refused to accept it out of fear that it might have been confiscated, and therefore there would be a stain of theft upon it. This matter further raised the honor of the rabbi in the eyes of the ruler. When this captain was appointed as the ruler of Zelovo, a relatively larger town, and its rabbinical seat became vacant, the ruler pleaded with him to accept the rabbinate of Zelovo, and promised that he would help him. However, to the astonishment of the captain, the rabbi refused to accept his advice and his assistance.

During the years 1919–1920, when the Polish authorities demanded that the rabbi turn over to them young Communists on the grounds that they had aided the Russians, the rabbi refused to do this, despite the threats by the Polish commander of a military judgment – which at the time implied the death penalty. The rabbi was saved only thanks to the intercession of the Catholic priest, his acquaintance and friend. The rabbi also did a great deal in the communal and educational realms. He was one of the activists in the Jewish banks and cooperatives of Poland. He participated in their conventions in Warsaw and Bialystock. He assisted the "Centus", the national association for the assistance of orphans. He was especially diligent regarding education in his city. A national–religious school was founded, which taught general subjects in additional to religious studies.

Even though he was not an official Zionist like his father–in–law Rabbi Pines, who was one of the leaders of Mizrachi, he was dedicated to the idea of the settlement of the Land of Israel throughout his life.

After Rabbi Y. Rozen left Svisloch, this position was offered to Rabbi Miszkinski. However the community of Konyuszany urged him not to leave, and the rabbi acceded to this request. Only two years later, when Rabbi Eidelberg left his position, did Rabbi Miszkinski answer the invitation of the community of Svisloch and accept its rabbinate.

In Svisloch as well, he was dedicated to communal matters, especially to national–religious education with an intermixing of holy and secular. He endeared himself simultaneously to the Orthodox and liberal circles.

During the Second World War

When the Soviet battalions entered the town, they issued a decree of expulsion to the wealthy refugees (there were indeed such). The rabbi interceded on behalf of the refugees so that they would not be expelled to the interior of Russia; a decree which was then considered a disaster. His intercession did not succeed, and they were expelled, which indeed saved some of them. They did not touch the rabbi himself to expel him, as had happened to other rabbis, for even the local

Communists did not accuse him. Thus, his bitter fate was to remain. At the time of the German conquest, he had the opportunity to flee to Vilna, however he listened to the instructions of Rabbi Chaim Ozer[1] to the rabbis of the region to remain with their communities. He witnessed its end, and his only consolation was that his two sons were in the land of Israel. In 1942, a few weeks before the end of Jewish Svisloch, the rabbi succeeded in sending a postcard to his eldest son Yitzchak in the land of Israel, through intermediaries in Turkey. Upon the postcard was a Nazi postage stamp with the visage of the devil may his name be blotted out, and on the other side was a few lines, which displayed nobility, self control, greatness of spirit and faith despite the anguish of the occupation. He ended with the words, "We have nothing upon which to rely except for our Father in Heaven".

On November 2, 1942, the Nazi human beasts murdered the majority of the Jews of Svisloch in the Visvanik Forest. The first to be murdered were the rabbi and his wife, Rebbetzin Yocheved. His youngest son, 21 year old Naftali Hertz, was among those imprisoned in the Bialystock Concentration Camp, where he was murdered. As was related by an eyewitness, the rabbi delivered a sermon before those who were to be murdered, and spoke about Sanctification of the Divine Name.

(This article is based upon an article signed by V. Ben–Ir in the book Eile Ezkera, Vol. 3.)

Translator's Footnote:

1. Grodzinsky, one of the leading rabbis of the era.

[Page 31]

Institutions of Torah, Education and Culture

By Ch. Sh. Rubin (Egosewicz)

Translated by Jerrold Landau

a. Traditional Education (cheders, the Talmud Torah, and their teachers)

From the time of Yehoshua ben Gamla, the High Priest who instituted "one must appoint teachers of children in each and every country, and in each and every city, and bring in the children when they are 6 or 7 years old"[1], there were teachers of children in all Jewish communities. As in those days when there were schools of the community and schools of individuals known as "The house of the rabbi", similarly in every community and in every generation there were communal institutions called "Talmud Torah" and private ones called "cheders". The communal ones served the poorer of the people, and were supported by the community. The private ones existed through the efforts of the teachers (melamdim).

Svisloch as well had a Talmud Torah that was located near the Beis Midrash. It has cheders in the private homes of the teachers, or in premises that were rented for that purpose. The status of the teacher was lowly, both from an economic and from a social perspective. This was particularly the case with the teachers of young children, from whom erudition was not demanded, and every good–for–nothing and poor person became a teacher. The higher level teachers were respected, for their knowledge of Torah earned them respect. Among the teachers there were those who were graced with knowledge and pedagogical skill.

My Teachers

Reb Gedalia Sender, was a splendid Jew with a pointed face and a good heart. He was far from strict. Within the span of a few months, he would teach a child how to read from the prayer book. As was the situation of the times, the reading was synthetic. The letters and vowels were pronounced and joined together to form words: kometz aleph, a, etc. With the strangeness of the language, the young age of the child, and the lack of any connection between this learning and the world of the child, the few months that it took to learn how to read from the prayer book is to be considered a very short time. One must also take into account the large number of students who studies with him, for the tuition was very low, and Reb Gedalia Sender had to provide food for his family. Taking into account all of these difficulties, one must attribute the achievements to the personality and pedagogical skill of Reb Gedalia Sender.

We loved him very much, and I will never forget the year that I studied with him. The memories are only pleasant.

What was the secret to the success of Reb Gedalia Sender? I state that it is his methodology. He was an individualist. One never heard shouts around his cheder, for he taught each child separately, as he sat and caressed the child on his cheeks and brightened his face. Each and every letter took on a meaning. The aleph was like Hershel the water drawer who carried a pole with two buckets of water over his shoulders. The beis was a house with an open door. The gimel was a poor lame man who was to be pitied. The non–final kaf was drawn like the foot of Moshe Matis. The shin was like a Sabbath candelabrum with three prongs. Reb Gedalia

Sender tried to make these associations. Others arose themselves in the child's imaginations. Who taught him this methodology? Not Farbel and not any other modern pedagogue.

He was able to practice his methodology because his cheder was hidden from the eyes of the householders who would have found fault in this methodology, since "the reward of a cheder is the shouting". His house bordered on the large garden of the wealthy Zvulun, which was more uncultivated than cultivated. The students of Reb Gedalia Sender would play there all day in shifts. Even during the brief intervals that they studied, the studies were accompanied by the caresses of the soft hand of Reb Gedalia Sender and his pleasant words.

I did not know him in his latter years, but as I have heard, he died at a ripe old age.

The Teacher from Molibod – Reb Zelig

Once I mastered the reading from the prayer book, I moved on to the teacher who taught me scriptures. Not every teacher had the good fortune to not be scrutinized by the householders. They did not particularly scrutinize the youngest children, but when the child started studying scriptures, serious study was demanded, study in unison, that would not only be listened to but also articulated, for the reading must be out loud. These teachers were for the most part very impoverished. Sometimes, they did not have room for the cheder in their simple houses, and they rented a dismal room.

The teacher who was appropriate for this age was Molibod. He had a reddish–brown beard, longer than usual. He was burdened with endless family difficulties: an insane son who would walk through the wide marketplace and throw stones skyward as he uttered meaningless shouts; and older daughters who were close to insanity.

Our cheder was dark and its floor was half rotted. We would spend most of our day in this room along with the rebbe. In the winter, it would be to the light of the lantern. Toward evening, his wife would bring him lentil soup in an earthenware bowl, which he would eat heartily, by placing the entire cup of the spoon into his mouth. I remember that I became accustomed to his style of eating, and I did not forget it for a long time.

Kindergarten

Despite the gloominess, the studies were not without sparks of light, for the material of study was Bible accompanied by his heartwarming stories, accompanied by explanations from Midrash. The forefathers came to life with the light of our being. Everything became real to us. The experiences and impressions of our surroundings became personified with the Biblical characters in a cloudy light. Our father Jacob sitting in the tents of Torah – something about him looking like the rabbi of the city. However, the picture became brighter when strength was added to him, "And when Jacob saw Rachel… he rolled off the stone from the mouth of the well". However, we did not understand the meaning of this strength, for what type of a stone would require all of the shepherds to gather together to roll it off?

Even the material in the Torah which is glossed over quickly in our time, such as the structure of the tabernacle, its vessels, and the priestly garments, was made pleasant by him no less than the stories. The treasure of the gold color, the blue and the purple, danced before the eyes of our imagination. How splendid and sublime was the image of the High Priest with the gold mitre on his forehead, with the breastplate and the apron intertwined with precious stones, with bells of gold at the hem of his clothes.

The enticing material atones for the external poverty, for the prolonged sitting without breaks, and for the continuous boring repetition.

With this, I loved my teacher Molibod and honored him. I was very anguished when I saw him in the Beis Midrash behind the podium and not on the east...

My Father of blessed memory (Reb Eliahu Horodner)

Reb Eliahu Horodner

When I started studying Gemara, I entered the cheder of Father of blessed memory. He was greatly honored, and was known as a great scholar and a scrupulously honest man. He was appointed as the trustee of a large charity and of the old Beis Midrash. He was even careful about separating out his own coins from the small coins in the charitable pot.

To his ill fortune, he ended up becoming a teacher. He hated teaching, and was strict in his teaching even though in conversations with friends he was pleasant and graced with a sense of humor.

Due to his righteousness, he never did his work with deceit. A student who did not know his studies would arouse his bitterness and ire. He would pour out the bitterness of his heart to the student, but even more so, he would pour out the bitterness to himself. The cheder was in his home – a large room divided with wooden partitions. In this house lived his 8 member family and Grandmother. The oven for heating and cooking was in the same room. Beneath the oven was a coup for several chickens that were being kept for kapparot[2]. I remember that before he bought this house, he lived in the dilapidated house of 'Alter Pinchas', where the situation was many times worse. It is easy to assume that one cannot be jealous of teachers who had to teach 8–9 year old children the Talmudic passages of the "ox that gores the cow" and "he who places a pitcher"[3] under such conditions.

Nevertheless, the learning took hold, for he did not accept more than nine students. That way, he would be able to concern himself with each student. Since the number of students was small, the tuition fee was high, and only children of the wealthy were accepted, or those who sacrificed the bread from their own mouths so that their children would master Torah.

There were several very good students in this cheder, who would arouse the jealousy of those less gifted. In addition, the Torah atmosphere that filled the home and the Beis Midrash, and the caresses and words of praise that were the lot of every good student inspired the students to study an excel, in such a manner that the dry discussion of the Gemara, spiced with the feeling of eternity, turned into a blessed vessel for those who were fitting, and something even stuck for those who were less fitting.

After time, he was appointed as a teacher in the Talmud Torah. The responsibility diminished, but the number of students increased. There were some children who were wild at home and wild in the cheder. All of this had an ill effect upon his health, and his upright and faithful heart stopped before its time.

Reb Moshe David was a teacher in the highest grade of the Talmud Torah. This was the highest level of study in the town. To go further, one had to go to a place of Torah. For what reason did Reb Moshe David merit this? It is hard to explain. Was it because of Torah? There were scholars of his level who worked in teaching, such as Reb Eliahu or Reb Zamah. It was because at this level, they no longer dealt with Gemara and Rashi, but entered into the ladder of didactics (pilpul), and Reb Moshe David had a sense of didactics. He did not satisfy himself with the didactics of the Tosafot. He enjoyed the Pnei Yehoshua. There were times when he would delve into the depths of the Pnei Yehoshua in class without being able to dig to the shore. Reb Moshe David would stand, with his splendid beard, swaying his entire body to and fro, as he smoked his cigarette and blew out streams of smoke, with the class in front of him. I imagine such a situation among our Sabras[4]... we were indeed righteous. There were individuals who were wild, but they received their punishments and calmed down.

Reb Moshe David's entire essence was Gemara. It was said of him that during the fair, he debated over the price of an egg with a gentile woman who asked for 4 groszy. He desired to play a joke, and he offered 2 kopecks (a kopeck is a coin worth 2 groszy). When the gentile, who did not understand, refused to accept, he told her in the tune of Gemara: "What is the practical difference, 2 kopecks and 4 groszy are indeed equivalent."

Translator's Footnotes:

1. A Talmudic quote.
2. A ceremony on the eve of Yom Kippur that involves swinging a chicken around the head.
3. Sections from the laws of torts in the Talmudic tractates of Baba Kama and Baba Metzia – among the most difficult talmudic sections.
4. A Sabra is a term for a native Israeli.

[Pages 36-44]

Sislevitch and its Teachers

by Eliahu Ayin

Translated by Joseph Rozenberg and William K. Rosenbloom

The Teacher, Aaron Isaac Ayin and his wife

Yedidya The Author, with a happy face and a very nice little trimmed beard, sneaked behind a young man who was sitting in front of the Post Office and grabbed a corner of the newspaper which the man was reading.

"Why are you grabbing the piece of paper," did my step-brother Aaron Isaac Ayin, the Russian Teacher call out with anger. "Tell me you want the paper! I will give it to you."

"I don't want the paper," explained Yedidya. "I only want the advertisement for the bottle of wine that is advertised there."

Every Shabbos afternoon, a lot of people, especially the young and intelligent, used to walk over to the Post Office at the end of Amstibover Street in Sislevitch, and when walking about used to carry a newspaper or magazine which arrived that day.

In the first decade of this century (1900), all the parents of children demanded that their children also get a secular education (in addition to a religious education); especially for the girls, because they never attended chader (religious school).

Yedidya was not a teacher and not an educator. He was in a special class of his own, between educator and teacher, with the title "Author".

He was greatly loved by his girl students and also by the Talmud Torah boys when he gave a class, one hour's time.

He used to entertain the children with jokes and anecdotes, which they used to enjoy very much.

The teaching was very easy and was mostly done by copying the answer with their own handwriting. After copying the answer for a few weeks, or maybe months, Yedidya used to give them another answer.

To a girl who was learning at his home where he had a class, he often used to tell her, "you, yourself, pick the answer." She used to walk over to the box of answers and pick one out; any answer she wanted; a short one, a middle sized one, or a long answer.

Aaron Isaac. He was a tall (man) with a nice built front and starched white cuffs, a bib, a starched collar with cuff links and a black top hat. His pride was in his brown mustache and pointy beard.

It was known that the Czar for a while expected that the Russian Language and its culture should all spread among the Jewish People.

Later on, they (the Russians) decided that it is better that the Jews should be less educated. Aaron Isaac, together with a few Jewish boys went through the later 80's (1880's) to the last century with a diploma as "First Class Jewish Teacher," a Jewish Private Teacher.

Until today (when this letter was written) if you meet somebody in America or Israel, a landsman from Sislevitch or a lady from Sislevitch, who learned Russian when she was young, if it's a him or a her, without exception, it was learned from Aaron Isaac.

In 1892, I was at his wedding to Zeesle Eisenstadt's in Volp. The father-in-law was a tall and well built man, a strong man. Once, a drunkard attacked him at the hardware stand (in the market). He took a horseshoe and bent it with his hand, and told the drunkard "you see now what I can make out of you." He told the farmer to shut up.

Another time, it happened at the time of the pogrom.

Two attackers became too bold. Eisenstadt took his one hand, took one attacker by the collar, and in his other hand the 2nd one. He carried them both out and dropped them to the ground.

One class Aaron Isaac held at the home of the town's Rabbi, Reb Shnearzalman.

Once when he taught the older children he noticed that in the corner was sitting a little boy about 5 years old, and he was listening to us. So Aaron Isaac asked him " What is more 2/3 or 3/3?" The little boy answered the right answer and proved that he knew as much as the older children had learned.

The little boy was Arka, the city rabbi's boy, the now famous scholar Reb Aaron Kotlar who is the head of Kletzker Yeshiva in New York.

The Rabbi's oldest child was Malka. They used to say that she knows how to write a good Hebrew. Just like Nachum Sokolov, and that she is a very nice and refined girl. She is now a medical doctor in Paris.

Aaron Isaac is now a very busy man with his classes, so much that he didn't have time to eat peacefully. On top of it, he was a very strict man. That is why there is no wonder that he had ulcers in his stomach. After 16 years of being a teacher he was forced to change his occupation---and became a cutter of horse hides in a leather factory.

And on top of it, he was a book-keeper. He was the head book-keeper and administrator in Sislevitch, at the Sislevitcher Dep't. of the Jewish Cooperative

Bank. And we Jews used to call it "Dos Benkele" where hundreds of Jews used to get loans at very small interest.

A Group of Teachers

Once it happened in the Amstibover Street Bet Midrash, by the trenches, a dispute broke out because of aliyoy (honors given for one to go to the Torah and give a blessing). Aaron Isaac went up to the podium and after the Cohayn and Levi, the first and second aliyot he told them to call the President of the Bet Midrash who sat on one side of the bench; after him they called up the 2nd person who sat on the 2nd place of the bench, and then the 3rd one. It didn't take long and they didn't fight over aliyot any more.

In the First World War, Sislevitch was occupied by different armies. When something bad happened, they used to run to Aaron Isaac. Once, they let him know that the Russian soldiers are looting Hershal Bozhik's store. Right away, he looked up the officer of the Army and stopped the looting.

The Germans drove out the Russians and made Aaron Isaac a peacemaker. The farmers used to say to the Jews, "You have it good with the Germans. You can talk to them". The farmers used the Jews to protect themselves from the German soldiers.

A German officer would stop a Russian or Polish farmer and tell him something. When the farmer didn't understand him he became angry. He would beat him without mercy.

As a peacemaker, Aaron Isaac protected everybody as much as he could. A lot of people thought he was dumb to do that for no pay. He could have made a lot of money for translating.

When the Polish People came back to power they made the Mayor of the town a Dr. Bittner. He was embarrassed the way the Polish Army took advantage of their new found freedom.

Chofetz-Chaim, from Raadio, Blessed Be He, once told to a Polish Minister (government official) "I saw once how the Russians led a group of Polish People handcuffed in chains. I cried when I saw it; and why did they deserve that? Because I thought they were fighting for their freedom, but now, when I see what they are using their freedom for and what they are doing with their freedom, I doubt that their freedom will last long."

The Minister told the translator that he did not need to translate into Polish; "that one heart feels another" (I understand what they say and feel).

When we used to hear loud sounds in town, we knew that the Polish Soldiers are looting and pulling beards (it was a common practice and way of humiliating Jews). So Aaron Isaac would run to Dr. Bittner for help.

For the short time, when the Bolsheviks were in Sislevitch, they cleaned out the town. The production and commerce stopped altogether. Everything was like dead. Everybody was enjoying their leaving town, more than any other occupiers.

Aaron Isaac's closest friend was Abraham the Pharmacist. Avramka Rothbart was some year in Krinik before he immigrated to Canada. In a short time, he made the license for Pharmacy. He was the first Jewish druggist in Toronto (maybe all of Canada) with whom the immigrants from Europe could talk to.

Very early on, Aaron Isaac started his career as a teacher in Russian together with Hebraist Shlomo Belkin and had a chader (school) in the market for girls who wanted to learn both languages. Belkin was a very restless skinny Jew. He was studying at the Mirer Yashiva but he didn't want to become a Rabbi. He was the local correspondent and contributor at the Petersburg Daily, "Hamaylitz". Almost all of the teachers were Zionists. The older ones were, of course, even before Herzl.

The first time I tried to read a number of the daily paper "Der Freind" I was embarrassed very much that, I, a little boy who could read already the Torah, had such a hard time reading a few lines in "jargon" (Yiddish).

Shlomo Belkin used to lend his own books to everybody with a desire to read. The first Hebrew book I read, I borrowed from him.

A son of his is now the famous Dr. Samuel Belkin, President of Yeshiva University of New York.

Shlomo Belkin was once in a cheder of a young teacher. He, the big Hebraist, admitted to himself, without shame, that he was jealous of the teacher; how he keeps order and discipline in his class.

The teachers name was Sukenik and he, later became the world famous Professor of Archeology at Hebrew University in Jerusalem.

Sukenik looked shorter than he really was, because of his wide built body. He belonged to the S.S. (Territorialists, Jews who advocated the establishment of an autonomous state other than Palestine) but was not active in it. My brother David, the ex S.S. man gave two possible reasons for this; the first one, as a teacher he couldn't be an outspoken revolutionary, and second, he was really a sympathizer of Poalei Zion (Zionist Socialist Party, which didn't exist in Sislevitch).

One time in Sislevitch, possibly in 1907, news arrived that a pogrom is going on in Bialystok. Sukenik's parents and family lived in Bialystok, and he became hysterical. They knew in Sislevitch what was going on. All of the town's people got together around the house of Gershon Slutzky, the leather manufacturer and Zionist, where Sukenik was also present.

I think another Sislevitcher man needs to be mentioned here, even though he is not a local teacher. Rav Shimon Langbard is a writer and also head of the Volozheener Yeshiva in Jerusalem. His family were neighbors of ours for many years.

His father would comb down his beard with an open palm to the pointed end of his beard and say "if I want, I'm Arye" and then he would go over his beard with a half open palm to the two points of his beard and say , "now if I want, I am 'Rav Arye' ."

One of the first Hebrew teachers was Shlomo Rozpinsky.

He made a good living.

He was married to a Sislevitcher girl.

The progress in town drew lots of teachers from out of town. Very few teachers were from Sislevitch. When there was a slowdown in the leather industry, Rozpionsky moved to Krinik.

The outstanding teachers were the ones brought to town by the Zionists Aaron Isaac, Gershon Slutzky, Pyshe The Forest Commissioner, and others who brought teachers for their own children.

His name was Kulik. Right away in the beginning he introduced teaching Hebrew in the Hebrew Language. After 2-3 semesters with him, his students conversed a good Hebrew on the streets of town. One student, a girl, was composing Hebrew songs. One song she wrote was "El Hatsipor." The famous author Abraham Reisen met her a few times in New York. Her name is Dobie Eden. She resides now in Tel Aviv.

The "old fashioned way" teachers were scared. They started to call the new way school, "dangerous chaders". Thereafter, all the Hebrew Schools had the same good success. It was the wonderchild of Chaim Brisker, the manufacturer, and owner of underwear and other knitted goods.

Chaim Bagon traveled to Brest especially to tell Rav Chaim Brisker about the new method of teaching; that you can teach a child in months what took earlier years to teach the same thing. But all that didn't impress Rav Chaim, since he believed that the new way of learning is the way of heretics.

Sucharevsky - he was really loved by his students, as is his last name's meaning in Russian; in reality he was dry bones and skin.

Yoshe Tzivie's, a grain dealer, an enlightened man in Hebrew and Russian, used to spend a few hours a week teaching at the Talmud-Torah. He came straight from his basement in dusty clothes to school and gives as good a lecture as any educator can.

Half teacher, half tutor, he was a middle-aged man from the town of Porozove. He dressed sportily. He wore also rings on his fingers. He also let his thumbnail grow as the style of the time, which very few people followed. The rumor was that he was in the process of writing a book.

Lurie was a good teacher in the Russian Language. He was handsome, delicate and educated. He tried his best to get in at a University, but for Jewish sophomores it was very hard to accomplish. He was doomed for life to stay at a teacher's level.

At the end, he married, became a father and practiced teaching in Sislevitch.

Schneider, a young Russian, the son of a widow and very handsome. He made a decent living by giving Russian classes to Jewish children. He did purposely work with Jewish students as time demanded. He was also a revolutionary. He told me that the S.S.nik's are Chauvinists, and that he would be indoctrinated by the Bundists[1]. But the Russian Socialists thought of the Bundists also as Chauvinists; because the Bundists program was just for national cultural autonomy.

By the way, the program of the Bund was voted down at their own conference. And when it was all over, the Bund Members still didn't realize what (had) happened.

I observed once how Velie Catzenelenboigen, the Zionist and red- headed lady Hebrew Teacher had a very hard time conversing in the Hebrew. All the time, she used the slogan "kemuvan" (which means self-evident), just like the bad Russian Teachers used often the expression "vobshtchay" which means "in general". At the same time, students from the new school system could easily converse a fluent Hebrew.

To finish this off, I must mention the Zionist and public servant Velie's husband Yoshka, the tall Catzenelenboigen who was instrumental in getting rid of all hindrance to bringing in a secular education for the Talmud Torah.

Signed Eliahu Ayin(Canada)

Translator's Footnote:

1. Jewish Labor Bund was defined as the Socialist Labor Party influential in Poland and other East European Countries until WWII. They did not believe in the necessity of a Jewish State, but believed Jews should be accepted in any land and allowed to live as Jews through Socialist ideals in the land they chose.

[Page 45]

The Modern Cheder

by N. Eden

Translated by Jerrold Landau

The Modern Cheder was a transitional phase between a cheder and a Hebrew school. It was founded in our town by a group of Zionist activists: Reb Yossel Katzenelboigen, Reb David Meisel, Reb Aharon Yitzchak Ayin, Reb Daniel Gershon Halperin, Reb Gershon Slutski of blessed memory, and others. It started out with the Hebrew in Hebrew methodology. It accepted students of the age of 6–7. The first teacher was Shlomo Rozpinski. The education was in the Zionist spirit. On Sabbath and festival eves, we heard Zionist speeches and sang Zionist songs, led by the teacher Rozpinski and Reb Yosef Katzenelboigen, who conducted enthusiastically with his baton.

In school, we spent most of the day in Hebrew and spoke among ourselves in Hebrew, which became fluent on our lips. This made an impression even on the opponents – the Orthodox, the traditionalists, and the avowed Yiddishists who were forced to acknowledge our success.

The teacher Rozpinski immigrated to England at the time of the Russo–Japanese war, and his place was filled by the excellent teacher Kulik, in whose classes an exemplary orderliness prevailed. During his time, the cheder was in the home of Reb David Meisel. The following served as teachers in the cheder: Lipa Soknik (later a professor in the Hebrew University of Jerusalem), the Maskil Shlomo Belkin, Mordechai Pelman, and Reb Yaakov Finkelstein who was known for his sharpness and sharp statements. The teacher Rozpinski returned to teaching at the end of the Russo–Japanese war. With the passage of time, the Russian language was also taught. The teachers of this language were Reb Aharon Yitzchak Ayin, Serlin, Arnonski, Luria, the engineer Rosenblum, Mrs. Glin, and others.

The modern cheder closed when the First World War broke out.

[Pages 46-49]

The Hebrew School in Svisloch

by Shimon Finkelstein

Translated by Jerrold Landau

The Public Hebrew School in Svisloch

Standing from right to left are the principals and teachers of the school: Reb Avraham Elkanitzki, Reb Chaim–Shlomo Shabzin, Yisrael Azerovitch, Naftali Eden, Yosef Katzenelboigen, Chaim Watnik, Kayla Eden, Alter Goldberg

Its History and Development

It began at the end of the battles of the First World War. Already in 1920, after the death of Yosef Trumpeldor, a memorial ceremony for him was conducted. The first school was established in the building that had formerly served as a hospital.

Hebrew education had already existed in the town in the form of cheders taught by the melamdim (cheder teachers). They were liquidated by decree of the Germans during the First World War, although remnants remained. Later, even they came to an end through a decree of liquidation. With the death of the most of the teachers, there was nobody to renew them.

However, a modern cheder was established even during the time of the cheders. As I have heard, it was coeducational, however I do not believe that the modern cheder served as a bridge between the cheders and the school.

Its Founders

The local Zionist activists founded the school. The most prominent of them was the veteran Zionist Reb Yosef Katzenelboigen, who served as the secretary of the school for many years. Practically, he was even more than this: he was its spokesman for the Land of Israel. His speeches on Tu Bishvat and on other holidays, emotional and stormy, brought him to shortness of breath. At times, he had to struggle strongly with members of the left who would disrupt. He spared no effort to instill a Zionist spirit into us. Through his personality, the Land of Israel was painted for us. Mr. Avraham Elkanitzki served as chairman of the school committee for many years.

The Teaching Faculty

From all perspectives, the image of the school was a result of a long period of development, and its curriculum was influenced by many sources. Religious studies had a recognizable role as a legacy from the cheders. The teacher Chaim Shlomo Shabzin was accustomed to the spirit of the times, and he was employed by the school as a teacher of religious studies for a few years. He taught prayers and Torah. The explanations were in Yiddish. Teachers of Gemara were specially invited. The rabbis had great influence on this matter. Rabbi Rozen was involved in this activity, and later Rabbi Miszkinski continued with even greater involvement. Prayers for the boys took place every day before the studies. The Torah trope was taught, and Pirke Avot (the mishnaic tractate of Chapters of the Fathers) was taught on the Sabbath. Rabbi Miszkinski examined the students. I still have a siddur (prayer book) that was given to me in recognition of my excellence in Talmud, signed by the rabbinate in 1929.

It is appropriate to note that the study of Talmud interested us, and I would bother my grandfather Reb David Meisel with questions. From his side, he exhibited patience to me and to my friends with regard to the Talmudic discussions that we brought forth. Evidently, he hoped that we would continue in our Talmudic studies.

The influence of the rabbinate met with a spirit of opposition from some of the activists, who wished to run the school along the lines of the Tarbut schools.

At first, the curriculum of the studies was not restricted. Along with the brief subjects, there were main in–depth subjects. The first graduating class was, as I recall, in 1925. At that time, Zalman Margolis, Pinchas Brzanicki and others graduated. They suffered from disadvantages when they continued their studies in the high schools.

The curriculum consolidated with the passage of time. The principal Brom put great effort into organization the school from a social perspective. He established an organization for children called Ezrat Achim. In this framework, they were trained in independent organization. A chairman, treasurer and secretary were elected. Meetings of the directors took place at set times, in which they deliberated about the various activities, including assistance to needy students. At the conclusion of their studies, the students published a booklet called "The Fruits of our Thoughts".

During the tenure of Brom, they began to distribute a cup of cocoa and a bun to the students on a daily basis. This was appropriate for the times, for there was no shortage of needy students at the time. In the upper grades, literary activities were arranged, and literary judgements were conducted on various topics. All of this was thanks to Brom, who earned the appreciation and love of the students. During his time, several classes graduated, starting in 1927. A significant portion of the students continued in higher studies in Volkovisk, Bialystock, Vilna and Grodno.

The principal Szlachter improved the protocols and curriculum of the school. He and his wife came from Congress Poland. His language was Polish, and he was particular about the teaching of the Polish language. We did not relate favorably to this language, but we nevertheless got used to the principal. He improved the external form of the school. He added physics and chemistry equipment. The level of the studies rose to the level that the school was able to measure up with any other school in the region.

In the realm of cultural life, the students of the school performed many performances in the fire hall. The income was dedicated to the development of the school. Its livelihood was based on the tuition fees that were progressive, so that the poor could study for free. An active parent organization also existed. My father was numbered among its members. When I concluded my studies at the institution, they arranged a goodbye party for him.

A well–furnished and orderly kindergarten existed alongside the school.

The Yiddish School

Grade 3 of the school and its teachers

Through the efforts of the supporters of Yiddish, a Yiddish kindergarten and school was established at the beginning of the1930s in Shacor's house on Rudbaka Street. Similarly, there was a Polish public government school in which some of the local children studied. Jews were not accepted to the government teachers' seminary in Svisloch, aside from a few exceptional cases. Of all these schools, the Hebrew school was the only one that educated in the spirit of Zionism and practical realization of aliya. Organizers of the local pioneering movement arose from amongst its graduates, and many made aliya to the Land of Israel. Had the way been open, all would have made aliya, for this was their sole desire.

From among the other cultural institutions, it is worthwhile to point out the two libraries, Hebrew and Yiddish. I estimate that they were founded at the beginning of the 20th century. The libraries were run on volunteer power, including for the binding of books. The activists in the library in the latter years included Sender Mintz and Zalman Margolis of blessed memory, and, may he live long, Tzvi Finkelstein.

Binyamin Lis worked with dedication in the Yiddish library.

[Pages 50-51]

Memories and Experiences from my Studies at School

by Shimon Finkelstein

Translated by Jerrold Landau

Children from grade 3 from the Hebrew primary school in Svisloch

I was accepted to the preparatory program in 1924. Our teacher was Dina Dorchinski. She was very particular that we sit with hands crossed over the chest (as she said, "Hands on the chests"), or crossed behind us. We had a non–local teacher in grades 1 and 2. I only recall her externals – short and dark, and her place of residence – with my uncle Finkelstein of blessed memory.

Brom was hired as principal when I was in grade 3. His personality was felt in the school. Alter Goldberg was our teacher in grades 4 and 5. We loved him and also made him angry.

Our class became consolidated starting from grade 6. The teacher was the wife of the principal Szlachter. We got used to her and related to her even though her language was Polish. I disparaged the study of the Polish language and claimed that I did not need it, since I expected to make aliya to the Land. She wanted to convince me that I should study Polish, with the reason that I would require it if I were to work in the Polish diplomatic corps, but I was not convinced. She worked very hard at educating us in social studies. She conducted discussions with us on these matters, and also arranged educational activities in this direction. She set up a mailbox in the classroom into which each student had the right to place letters of complaint, advice, thoughts from the heart, or social difficulties.

At the end of our sixth year of study, we published a wonderful booklet called "The Fruits of our Thoughts", of course in the Polish language. I still have it.

In the final grade, grade 7, she worked to prepare us for life. We dealt with many problems in social studies. We concluded that year as well with a fine booklet.

On the day of graduation and the distribution of report cards, we arranged a party with the parents. We then went to spend the night in the Vishbanik Forest.

Who would have imagined that in this place, the cord of life of the many Jews of Svisloch would be cut off by the accursed enemy, and that the grave of our dear parents would be there, after they were tortured and murdered with cruelty.

[Pages 52-55]

My Town Svisloch

by Yaakov Niv

Translated by Jerrold Landau

I stretch the eyes of my spirit and see it spread out before me as it was when I left it in 1921 to make aliya to the land of Israel. It was so pleasant with its streets, markets, houses, fields, institutions, and residents. I, as all residents of the town, knew them all. I knew their status and their nature, with their weaknesses and fine points. There was no shortage of plutocrats and wealthy people, fine people who lived in proper stone houses, as there was no shortage of desperately poor people who withered away in their agony. However, they were all dear to me – for all of them were graced with the authentic Jewish soul, which united them all and merged them together into one unified body. They bore all the conditions and situations with purity and faith, and they created mutual benefit organizations out of concern for the future.

They were immersed in all aspects of the struggle for existence, but with all this, they bore the yoke of Torah. Complete ignoramuses were rare in the town. Everyone studied until a certain age, and many continued to delve into Torah to an even older age. I will commence my description from the marketplace, and you will forgive me if I begin with my father Reb Daniel of blessed memory. His small store served as a gathering place for tens of Jews who would gather each morning for Torah and to discuss the matters of the day. One could hear lively discussion about what was transpiring in world politics, and later, about issues of life in the city: Zionism, the workers movement, and finally literal words of Torah – a novel idea that my father or someone else discovered in Halacha, and idea that came to the fore in a Talmudic section, on Rashi's commentary on a verse in the Torah, and the like. During the protracted conversation, words of gossip were also not absent (my father was revolted by words of gossip). Finally, the first customers would peer in and be embarrassed to enter because of the guests. My father was often angry in his heart about the guests who at times disturbed him from his livelihood, but he never said anything to them, until they themselves realized that they had to leave the store.

In our neighborhood was 'Zadnowitz' store, the store of the intelligentsia, where they often spoke the vernacular. Behind it was the house of Rubin and his children who introduced me to the Hebrew language… Eden's store, a family that was completely devoted to Hebrew culture… Azerovitch's store… and Lisin's flour store. The family was forsaken in its externals, but completely saturated with Torah and knowledge. His son Matot (Matchked) became one of the leaders of the Bolsheviks immediately after the Bolshevik conquest. He did me a favor by taking me under his protection and giving me a job so that I could earn a bit of money for our extended family. Later, he fired me in anger because I spoke to him in Yiddish rather than Russian, and called him by his first name and not Comrade Lisin. There was the house of the extended Meisel family, the Nazovitches, the Mintzes, the Finkelsteins, and the Schreibmans… all of these I remember, precious people of grace…

Behind the synagogue courtyard there were three structures – the old Beis Midrash, the new Beis Midrash, and the splendid synagogue. There I grew up, and there I studied Torah throughout the years. The old Beis Midrash was the house of worship of my father of blessed memory. It was a place of Torah and mitzvos. To the right of the Holy Ark was the seat of Rabbi Yosef Rozen during my time. Along the wall was a row of the city notables, opposite them were rows of lecterns, and tables surrounding the Torah reading table, running as far as the two heating ovens. At one of these tables I studied Talmud with my "friend" Reb Moshe, who was 50 years old (and I was 12!). By the tables near the ovens until the "Lizanka", groups studied Talmud and Mishna, dedicated themselves to the mysteries of the

Talmudic discussion, freed for a brief moment from their worries of livelihood. The melody that accompanied them in their studies still echoes in my ears, just as the similar melody of my father as he studied his page of Gemara in the early hours of the morning still rings in my soul. The small rooms behind the oven were the places where I studied Torah from the mouths of Reb Eliahu Egosevitch and Reb Chaim Shlomo. The women's gallery was the place of the cheder of the Velfer teacher, from whose mouth I obtained knowledge along with my friends who were older then I – Yisrael Azerovitch and Yeshayahu Slutski.

There were the "vigils". On every Thursday night at midnight we would stop our studies and go Bordosz's bakery to purchase fresh buns and pastries. We would then return to our studies. In the morning, we would play with buttons, and we would often go around with pants tired with a rope, as we had removed the buttons for the game. I also recall the ice cellar next the Beis Midrash. We would wait for the ice porters so that we could grab the chips that scattered outside.

In the winter, we would skate on the frozen slope between the synagogue and the old Beis Midrash! After the skating, we would divide into two groups and have a snowball fight. We would remain there until the fathers came to take us home, and then we would walk with glass lanterns in our hand.

At the side of the old Beis Midrash was the new Beis Midrash, the place where Reb Shmuel Malshinker was the gabbai. I could clearly hear the sounds of prayer from the Beis Midrash in my house. For some reason, we had no relationship with this institution. It seemed as if a secular atmosphere pervaded there, in contrast to the old Beis Midrash. Prayers on Sabbaths and festivals concluded there at an earlier time. In the dispute between the two "sides" there was the majority who cleaved to Yosef Rozen the "city rabbi", and the minority who opposed him. The people of this Beis Midrash had less attachment to the "city rabbi" than those of the old one. The spirits were stormy in this dispute. Even I, a youth, was caught up in this, even though I did not understand the situation clearly.

In the center was the synagogue in all its glory. Services were only conducted there on Sabbaths. On weekdays, they worshiped in the side rooms called the "shtibelach". I still remember the decorations of the dome of this building. For years they worked to beautify the synagogue. Expert cantors were invited to beautify the services. A cantor was selected after many examinations by people who understood music. The experts were specifically from the working class of the town: the builder, the butcher, etc. Nevertheless, people did not stream to this sanctuary. A coldness permeated it, and the old timers preferred to worship in the Beis Midrash. Even we children did not enjoy sitting in it. We sufficed ourselves with a brief interval, to listen the cantor for a bit. Services in this synagogue lasted longer than in the other houses of worship, for the cantor would elongate things. Finally, the Beis Midrash on Amstivova Street should be mentioned. It served that street and the "Okopes", which was sort of a poor neighborhood in the town. For some reason, the fortune of this Beis Midrash was poor, and it did not merit the honor and splendor that was befitting of it on account of its pleasant interior form.

It is worthwhile to note the bathhouse that was behind the synagogue courtyard. We visited this house every Friday and enjoyed the warm, pleasant vapors, the scrubbing of the back with twigs, as we lay on the steps naked as on the day of our birth, absorbing the warm vapors that came from the glowing stones in the oven as buckets of cold water were poured over them. I was happy when I was honored with the pouring of water from the bucket onto the stones.

In the summer we would pass by the bathhouse without paying attention. We walked on to the river. There, there was a section for women and a section for men. People swam without bathing suits, and if the eye peered into the wrong place, the hand would strike the breast with Al Chet[1].

The town was permeated with Zionism and Hebrew culture. Even the elders never ceased from praying on behalf of Zion. They dedicated their deeds to hasten the redemption. There were also members of the Bund who rejected Zionism and advocated for Yiddish, but the decisive majority was committed to Zionism in its different factions. They struggled greatly with the opponents. I recall Mendel Wigonski, an enthusiastic Bundist, organizing the tannery workers and publishing a bulletin. We desired some fun, and we sent " The Small Angel" of Frishman to their newspaper, signed by one of our members. They printed it with this signature, which mocked their glory, for they were experts in literature.

The various Zionist organizations united into a common organization called "The Center for Zionism". This center established a Hebrew school. Even the rabbi of the city participated in its establishment. It was located in the old hospital building in the synagogue courtyard. Reb Chaim Shlomo taught Torah and Mishna there, and the writer of this article taught history and math. There were also the teachers Goldberg, Levkovski, and Berlinkovski. A Hebrew library was established in the attic of Reb Shmuel Malshinker. Groups were created for the speaking of Hebrew, and a wide branched pioneering movement sprung up, affiliated with the central pioneering organization of Bialystock and with the center in Warsaw. Keren Kayemet stamps were distributed. It is worthwhile to point out the first and foremost of our teachers and rabbis, the head of the Zionist organization in our town Reb Yosef Katzenelboigen. He and his wife spoke only Hebrew between themselves. We also were careful to speak only Hebrew. The rest of the factions were also active: there were meetings, deliberations, debates, and above all else – a theater troupe. They set up a hall and performed Goldfaden's plays: the Witch, Mirele Efrat, and others. We also performed "The Sale of Joseph", "Saul and David".

Thanks to the Zionist activity, many of the townsfolk were saved, for they left the town and made aliya while there was still time. Among those who yearned for

Zion were the poor, despite their depressed economic and social situation. Many of them were known by nicknames such as: pepper, chicken, gnome, and telegraph, due to some event or another. Even this stratum of the people was enthusiastic about the efforts for the upcoming redemption. They were the first to send their children to Chalutz and to donate to the Zionist funds. On November 2, at the time of the Balfour Declaration, joy enveloped everyone. The city took on the air of a festival. The Beis Midrashes were teaming with people Blue and white flags decorated every house.

After I left the town, news came to me about the continuation of the activities. Father of blessed memory refused to accede to my request to make aliya, lest he fall as a burden upon the shoulder of his children. He continued to describe to me the life in the town, the innovations that took place there, and the people who had made aliya or prepared to make aliya.

Alas! The fate of Polish Jewry in general was the fate of my townsfolk. The hand of the evil executioners, may their names be blotted out, struck them. The natives of Svisloch will bear in their hearts and souls the memories of fathers and mothers, brothers and sisters, sons and daughters. A father will tell his child about the preciousness and splendor of the holy brethren who fell as Jews upon the altar of their people. May their memories be blessed.

Translator's Footnote:

1.   The Yom Kippur confessional.

[Pages 56-58]

From My Memories in One Article

by Naphtali Eden

Translated by Jerrold Landau

The Hechalutz Organization

In memory of the soul of my sister Dina and her family who perished in the Holocaust.

Forty–one years ago.

It was an era of ideals that were nurtured from the love of Zion on the one hand, and the progressive movement in Russia on the other hand.

I was the secretary of the Zionist and Hebrew cultural movement in the town. (I still have a list of the 24 members of the Herzliya group that formed the kernel of the Young Zion Organization, Svisloch branch. Beneath the list is the date February 19, 1919, and the seal.)

Our headquarters were in the home of Chaim Epstein. The different groups gathered there: to study Hebrew, to read Hebrew newspapers, the dramatic club, the music club, and others. At the time of an approaching election to the communal council there was also a municipal club. We prepared for defense, out of fear of pogroms due to the preparations of the Germans to empty the town. We received several guns from the Germans. I recall Avraham Ayin of blessed memory appearing with his gun on his shoulder.

Our office was a regional office, for the Germans made decrees on Svisloch as on the entire region, and we were able to provide use of organization and cultural forces for the entire area. Indeed, people from the region turned to us regarding matters of security and culture.

We debated a great deal with the Bundists: Berl David Ayin, Yosef Auerbach, Moshe Lash and others. They too were idealists. Moshe Lash immigrated to Canada and his son Louis is the head of the workers' movement there.

The funeral of the teacher Chanoch Minsky

From among the finest of the veteran Zionist orators, the following should be noted: Reb David Meisel of blessed memory, Reb Aharon Yitzchak Ayin of blessed memory, Reb Gershon Slutski of blessed memory, Reb Avraham Elkanitzki may G–d avenge his blood, Reb Daniel Gershon Halperin of blessed memory, and others. Through the efforts of these people, the Hebrew School was founded. Reb Alter Goldberg, Mordechai Pelman, Reb Chaim Shlomo Shabzin,

Chanoch Minsky who died of typhus, my sister Dina may G–d avenge her blood – a graduate of educational courses in Warsaw, and serves as a kindergarten teacher and teacher of the younger grades – and, may they live, Yaakov Halperin and the writer of these lines all served as the first teachers at this school.

Children of the towns and villages of the region streamed to the school. This increased our influence on the entire region. All of this wide branched work was performed voluntarily, and in the light of our era, it seems as if this was a dream.

The following is a list of the members of the Herzliya Group:

Moshe Bratnovski, Shmuel Meisel, Shimon Vatnik, Moshe Rubin, Pinchas Meltz, Naftali Eden, Yeshayahu Slutski, Moshe Satur, Yisrael Azerovitch, Feivel Zaionce, Zeidel Fuchs, Nachman Aleksandrowski, Perl Mintz, Sara Walski, Mordechai Halperin, Yehoshua Muchnik, Tzipora Epstein, Efraim Zadnovitch, Leib Lew, Leib Stopaczewski, Eliezer Shevelevitch, Doba Rubin, Pnina Zadnovitz, Kalman Slapak.

[Pages 59-62]

Sislevitch Enlighteners

by Elijah Ayin, Montreal

It says in the Book of Ethics (Talmud) "If there is no bread there is no Torah". When one makes a living and on top of it also has peace, then there is Torah, and of course, knowledge.

Sislevitch, Grodno Gubrnia, has in the first decade of this century (20th), enjoyed an economic boom from the income generated by the leather industry. This called out a jealousy from the neighboring towns, who called them (Sislevitchers) "Little Warsaw".

Because characteristically it is the same in other towns and cities, I believe that the Sislevitch Enlighteners deserve to be written about. Chananya Ourbach, skinny and very agile, was just the opposite of the slowpoke Leibee Matles. Leibee Matles humbly knew very much geography, geometry and other sciences, and without using the maps at hand followed every move of the Russian–Japanese War of 1904–05. They used to always argue and discuss everything that went on there. They felt there was no danger that their arguments would be reported by an informer to the authorities.

When the most important fortress at Port Arthur fell, the Russian Czar, a little person, and a big monster, didn't get to put this news in his daybook (diary). On the other hand in his daybooks he put what he had for dinner and what luck he had hunting. But not so relaxed were our two strategists. When news came to Chananya in the middle of the night, he went straight away, pounded on the window and cried out to Leibee, "Port Arthur fell"! I doubt they could continue to sleep that night.

Just as Leibee Matles didn't have any use for his knowledge, a lot of the educated Enlighteners had a lot of science knowledge but did not practice it. Prominent was the family of Berensteins. The father, Meyer, was very knowledgeable in science and literature, as well as in Yiddish and secular. For every occasion, in studies and meetings, he used the right and most interesting words. Once he explained the spirit of Joshua, the prophet: "There will come a time when all the jails will turn to schools, and penitentiaries into middle schools."

The second from the youngest son, Myshka (Mosha), used to play chess all the time. From time to time they would arrange contests and Myshka played 10 sets of chess against 10 contenders. At that time, when everyone had to bring their own chess board, Myshka would sit in another room. We, who used to help him, would come and report (to him) that certain contenders had made certain moves from one square to another.

He would then have us tell them (the contenders) what move he would make. Seldom did he lose a game.

Once, when they were young boys, Myshka and his present brother–in–law, Haskell Arleen from Montreal, got together to learn a page of the Talmud. Suddenly Myshka said, "I envy you".

Haskell asked, "How can it be? You know a lot more of the Talmud than I do."

[Page 60]

Myshka answered him. "It's true I know more than you–but you know more the depth of it than I do".

Haskell is still thinking to this day that this was the best compliment he ever received.

Yoshe Dretcheeiner, the merchant of textiles, was Berenstein's father–in–law. He was the only merchant (in the market) who would never use an oath when dealing with customers. (Some sellers might say something like, "I swear on my children's life that this is the best cloth in the world," and this is the way they advertised and drew customers.) Everybody believed him (Dretcheeiner) on his word. The way he did business was by purchasing a piece of material and charging his cost for a suit plus a 10% profit.

When another dealer used to use an oath ("on my honor") people used to answer him, "Just like the Shalom Aleichems' heroes. I believe you without the oath."

A researcher, a mystic and a self–made philosopher was Shimon the Beerer. He studied a few books but was in constant contact with the intelligencia. Meyer Berenstein also made a big impression on him.

When they discussed religion with the Polish priest they used to change the subject as soon as the priest's niece came in. Because this is the way they did it in Poland. They kept his niece to run the house.

Talking once with the Russian Greek Orthodox priest he asked, If you would be a Jew, what would be your opinion about being a Jew with the knowledge you have now?" The priest answered, "I would be hanging to Judaism with all my strength".

We should not forget that the Greek Orthodox religion at that time was not much better than Paganism: full of libels against Jews. Its real boss was not the Archimandrite or a Metropolis (Church Official) but an officer appointed by the Czar and not a religious person. The Prosecutor from the Holy Synod was called Pobedonostsev, a terrible creature in Russia, and was appointed by the Czar. The name meant "The Carrier of Victory", but we used to call him, Bedonostsev, "The Carrier of Misfortune."

As I can see it, the only ones who benefited from the Greek Orthodox religion at the time were the idiots. Just like the Moslem religion. Spiritual people are supposed to be possessed with the Holy Ghost. That's the way the masses of the Greek Orthodox believed. The idiots are supposedly possessed by the third person of the Holy Trinity, the triple of godliness, the Holy Ghost. That's why the Russians were good to the idiots.

Rachmiel the Teacher, a skinny one, with an intelligent friendly look, was a teacher with a logical mind. They used to call him often for arbitration between the lumber dealers.

Esther Rachael's Motke was a stutterer. He used to go for months proof reading, editing, and preparing the books for press, which, somewhere, a Rabbi had written.

[Page 61]

In great poverty, in a dark attic in the town hall, west from the famous big market, there lived Israel Zaam. Very close by the little panes of the window, with a yarmulke on his head. He was always sitting, very deep into reading science books and especially astronomy. When he was young, he shared his eagerness for science with Chaim Zalek Slominsky who later became an astronomer and publisher of the Hebrew Newspaper "Hatzfeyrah."

They used to tell stories that the Russian Government had announced it would give a big prize to one who would invent something which would measure the alcohol content in drinks. Israel Zaam sent in his invention, which he invented. And it was for the same invention which won the prize money, but his came in a day late.

One boy, a diplomat, but not educated in diplomacy was Kopl Rubenstein from Amstibover Street. Abraham Ayin from New York was the father–in–law of his (Kopl's) cousin, Avramtcha Mosha Nissen. Ayin, since the Second World War, had been tireless and accomplished so much in finding helpless refugees from Sislevitch's surrounding areas and connected them to their relatives in America.

Kopl: He was a tall, very nicely built man, with long vertical lines on his beautiful face, surrounded with cut red hair and a pointed little French beard on his chin. He always carried with him the look of an easy going, understanding and in a good mood person.

The name Rubenstein, like any other surname, we heard very often. We used to call him "Kopl the Redhead". He mostly used to negotiate with the clerks of the Russian Government. He was cold blooded, smart and experienced. He understood well where and how much to give for a bribe. He talked Russian not only fluently, but also a literate Russian. Once, when he needed to seal a contract to build a school, he started to look in all his pockets and said without his glasses he is an invalid. He signed it. At the end the clerk looked at the signature and said, "It looks like sticks and spades," then he looked at Kopl, then again at the signature, and in excitement he said, "I thought you were a highly educated person."

So Kopl answered, "First, without my glasses, I do not see how to write and second, my father was always a poor man and he was not able to provide me with an education."

In Sislevitch, a Polack doctor (M.D.) practiced since he graduated. His name was Linde: he was loved by the Jews and so assimilated with them he talked a perfect Yiddish, even with all the Hebrew words used in Yiddish. When he used to tell a sick Jew that he cannot fast on Yom Kippur, he used to tell him, "Just take small bites and small sips of the soup." Linde knew this was the Jewish Law. During Linde's funeral Kopl stopped the whole procession in the market and made a eulogy for him in Polish. Kopl knew the power of his language and he loved to see what else he could do with it.

[Page 62]

One time to the grain dealer, Yosha Tsivia, came a friendly Pole farmer with his old mother and brought him (Yosha) an arbitration case to handle. And it was about food. And Yosha called his neighbor and it was Kopl.

Kopl started to interview the mother and son in Polish, a rotten dialect of the Russian language: so wide ranging and so detailed (were the questions) that they both started to cry. At the end they both were crying. They hugged each other and cried harder and stopped arguing.

Kopl had a contract to supply horses to deliver the post (mail) to other towns and villages. One summer day, early in the morning, his son heard a noise in the direction of the horse barn. He jumped off the bed and ran outside. He had time to see 2 people run away on the post horses. Barefooted, he started to run after and followed them, over the little streets and gutters, and past the tanneries. Between the thieves you could find Jews——but horse thieves are only Poles. Back he came riding one horse and leading the other horse by hand.

[Pages 65-67]

Communal Life in Svisloch in our Generation

by David Zilberblatt

Translated by Jerrold Landau

Svisloch was a small, quiet town until the final years of the 19th century. Its Jewish residents supported themselves primarily from business and crafts, such as shoemaking, tailoring, carpentry, etc. The sons did not learn a profession, for this was considered as a lessening of their honor. They were supported by their parents, were somewhat part of the intelligentsia, went about idle, and spent their times on wantonness.

When the industry of the town began to develop, a new wind blew through the town. The sons of the householders began to study tanning.

In the wake of the decrees against the Jews and their expulsion from the villages, those expelled moved to the towns. They also joined the group of shopkeepers since they had no professions; however the industry that came to the town helped them from their straits. At first, gentiles from the surrounding villages were engaged in the working of hides. This improved the business situation, for there was more trade. However, with the passage of time, there was also a change with respect to the Jews. They began to realize that even though the economic situation had improved, there would be no permanence in this improvement if the industry remained in the hands of the Christians, and the livelihood of the Jews would be supported by naught. Therefore, people of the town began to stream to various types of industry. In the year 1900, with the additional development of industry, tradesmen from other places came to our town. There were for the most part influenced by the Bund[1], which was popular among the Jews.

The Bund had great influence on the circles of workers due to their battle for the improvement of the conditions of the workers. The ideology of the Bund also penetrated into the circles of workers. Our youth, who were educated in the nationalistic spirit, did not make peace with the ideology of the Bund. Their exclusive offer of protecting the conditions of the workers was also not particularly attractive. A united national feeling increased in light of the anti–Semitic feelings of the Russians and Poles. We realized that first of all, we must penetrate into all branches of the tanning industry. After a short time, we achieved an important place, and we tried to bring members of the Socialist Zionists and Poale Zion to the workplaces. Our influence grew among the workers thanks to the fact that the owner of the Mintz factory married off his daughters to two enthusiastic Zionists: Binyamin Minkes and Efraim Zadnowicz, who assisted him in his work.

We began to conduct political activity in the spirit of Poale Zion and Socialist Zionism. I recall one incident when we invited Chodikow to our town. He spoke wonderfully. The whole town was astir after his Zionistic speech. The Bund asked for a public debate and we agreed. The public assembly took place at the residence of Reb David Meizel. Aside from Chodikow, the veteran Zionist Yosef Katzenelboigen, David Meizel and other influential young people participated. They invited influential people from outside, over and above the local people. These included Moshe Bernstein, the grandson of Reb Yosef Drazner. As a result of the debate, our organization strengthened, and we started to conduct widespread activity on behalf of the Keren Kayemet and Keren Hayesod. It is important to point out that the Aguda[2] also opposed us and disturbed our efforts. To our good fortune, the rabbi of the city was at the time Rabbi Moszkinski, who was the son–in–law of Rabbi Pines of Bialystock – a veteran Zionist who supported us. I began to work in the tanning factory in 1902. I began to study the trade of cutting. I began to earn an income, and I left my parents' home. I rented a dwelling along with the teacher Serlin who was also a member of Poale Zion, and I dedicated myself to work with the movement. Most of the meetings took place in our room in an illegal fashion. We printed propaganda flyers. I would travel to Bialystock on occasion to bring publicity material. I was successful, and I never once failed.

The committee of the Keren Kayemet (Jewish National Fund)

Public life in the town developed well. A Hebrew school was founded, with the curriculum of the primary schools. We brought in teachers from outside. They had an understanding of Zionism and conducted a wide range of activity. They assisted in the education of the younger generation, who were instilled with the spirit of nationalism and Zionism.

Later, two important forces joined us. These were Avraham Eiliknicki, who was a fine organizer and good speaker, and Dr. Meizel who was also one of the important Zionist activists. Similarly, Binyamin Minkes and Efraim Zadnowicz were also very dedicated to the movement. Thanks to them, we penetrated all strata of the community, and had all of the movements joint us in action: including Poale Zion, the general Zionists and Mizrachi. Of course, the ideological deliberations and debates did not let up. However, the main task – canvassing the community for the Keren Kayemet and Keren Hayesod, was conducted in a joint fashion.

At first it was customary to enlist the help of the schoolchildren for canvassing, but I insisted that the adults should also help in the effort. This was for the best, both from a Zionistic educational perspective and also from a financial perspective.

We also helped to our fullest extent the advisors and speakers who came from outside. We developed a widespread activity, and did not pass up on any opportunity. We arranged an activity for the benefit of the Land of Israel at every holiday and festive occasion.

With the passage of time, an understanding of Zionism penetrated to most of the strata of the community, primarily to the young generation who had already been educated on the knees of Zionism.

The activities of Hechalutz began to move toward actualization and aliya to the Land. Several families made aliya. In 1926, my son Reuven, who was a member of Hechalutz, made aliya.

Pioneers for Hachsharah[3] began to arrive in Sviloch. We received them pleasantly, and attempted to set them up with work in the factories, primarily in tanning and in the sawmill of Kalman Slapak. At the time, I was the foreman in the tanning factory of Bendet Meizel and his sons. I accepted several male and female pioneers (Chalutzim) to work. The Bund looked upon our activities with a bad eye, and hatched some plans to foil us. They demanded the owners to fire the Chalutzim and hire others in their stead. The owners, who were Zionists, were undecided, however I stood my own. The Bund then declared a strike, and the owners came to me with the complaint that this bad situation was my fault. However, I offered them the choice – them or me. The workers returned to work after three days, and the matter ended with the opinion of the community on our side.

In praise of our town we should point out that in general, the townsfolk were good people, imbued with a sense of responsibility. They participated in all charitable institutions: Bikur Cholim, Gemilat Chesed, Linat Tzedek[4], and others.

In 1934, when the anti–Semitic spirit began to blow through Poland and reached our city as well, I understood that I had no place in Poland, and I began to prepare for my aliya to the Land of Israel. I made aliya. To my great anguish, my friends remained there, and the evil hand, may its name be blotted out forever, annihilated them. Their memory will not depart from us.

Translator's Footnotes:

1. A secular, non-Zionist, left wing Jewish movement.
2. A non-Zionist orthodox movement.
3. Hachsharah is a term for preparations for making aliya.
4. Bikur Cholim is visiting the sick, Gemilat Chesed in the granting of charitable loans, Linat Tzedek is the provision of shelter for wayfarers.

[Page 68]

The Beginning of the Young Zion (Tzeirei Tzion) Party in Svisloch

by Yitzchak Dov Egosewicz

Translated by Jerrold Landau

I remember when I was still a young child. At the beginning of the 20th century, there a recognizable Zionist movement existed in Svisloch, that stood out in nationalistic education, Hebrew culture (with the modern Cheder), a Hebrew library, and donations and canvassing for the Keren Kayemet Leyisrael through plates on the eve of Yom Kippur in the synagogue. The prominent activists were Reb Yosef Katzenelboigen, Reb Moshe Tzvi Watnik (the Siberian), and Aharon Yitzchak Ayin. The Hebrew teachers were Shlomo Belkin and Yechezkel the son–in–law of Akiva Ayinbinder. From among the young activists, I remember Avraham Eiliknicki, Minkes, the teacher Alter Goldberg, and others. All of these were for the elderly or young adults. On the other hand, I do not remember strong Zionist activity among the youth. The situation became extinguished at the beginning of the First World War and the German occupation. Only toward the end of the war, particularly after the Balfour Declaration, did the movement awaken amongst the youth. At that time, a Zionist club opened in the home of Chaim Epstein. Lectures on literature and personalities of the movement took place every evening. We conducted debates. The following were among the activists of the youth: Chaim and Shimon Watnik, Eizerowicz, and Reuven Egosewicz. The primary aim was Hachsharah and preparations for aliya to the Land. This continued until the 1920s, particularly 1921. During those years, with the first disturbances in the land and the closing of aliya, the movement dwindled recognizably among the youth. Some of the activists left Svisloch, and the rest struggled fiercely with the Bundists and Communists, who raised their heads at that time with the successes of the Bolsheviks in establishing their rule. A strange situation was created: even though in truth most of the Zionist members were from among the families of the householders, tradesman, small scale shopkeepers and workers – all from the non–wealthy classes – the Zionists identified with the bourgeoisie at all opportunities, such as in the elections for the Polish Sejm. This was because the factory owners were the leaders of the Zionists, whereas the Bund was considered the sole representative of the workers and poorer strata of the population. Therefore, we saw the need to found a left wing Zionist organization that would be able to measure up the Bundists.

This took place around 1922. A small number of people gathered together, including Naftali Eden, Shmuel Watnik, Knacipolski, Krabcki, and the writers of these lines. After deliberating for a short time, we decided to found a Socialist Zionist party. We immediately established contact with the center in Warsaw, received directives from there, and acted in accordance with the directives. We would meet several times a week, and study the literature and problems of the Land of Israel. Aside from the aforementioned objectives, the main objective was aliya to the Land. As time went on, more members joined us. In our wake, the Berezanicki brothers went out and founded Hechalutz. Together, this encompassed several dozen members, perhaps most of the youth of Svisloch. After I had made aliya, I heard that members came from outside the city to prepare themselves for aliya in Svisloch.

Most of the aforementioned people were murdered by the Nazis, may their names be blotted out.

[Pages 69-70]

The History of Zionism in our Town

by Feivel Zaonce z"l

Translated by Jerrold Landau

The Zionist movement was not organized in our town until the First World War. We made mention of the Land of Israel in our prayers, and there were charity boxes for Rabbi Meir Baal Haness and the Ground of the Land of Israel in the home of my teacher Rabbi Chaim Shlomo. He had a small bag of earth in his snuffbox. He would stroke his brown beard with his hand and say: "This is holy earth, which awakens the feelings of the holiness of the Land in our imagination."

From a cultural perspective, there were two groups – the Hebraists and the Yiddishists. Each of their activities was limited to the maintenance of a library of about 200 books. The groups were not adversarial to each other. Each group attempted to educate their children in accordance with their spirit; however, in general, most of them received their education from the cheders. There were no schools, and when Y. Finkelstein attempted to set up a modern cheder, he did not succeed.

However, this elder Zionist did not merit to make aliya to the Land and to witness the birth of the State.

[Pages 71-73]

"Before the Candle of G–d is Extinguished"

by Naphtali Eden

Translated by Jerrold Landau

Houses of Prayer

These were the focal point for the religious and national life of the Jews, and therefore, they and their contents were guarded as an especially valuable possession. If the Beis Midrash excelled in its inside form, with its rich religious library and quality of its students, the synagogue was a symbol of the Temple, and therefore an attempt was made to bring its external splendor into its walls. Thus was the synagogue in our town.

Aid for Orphans

The synagogue was burnt along with a large portion of the town in 1910. Reb Yosef Katzenelboigen was very active in its rebuilding. He went abroad for this purpose to collect money from the natives of our town, which would be used to build it up and beautify it. By chance, a professional artist passed through our town, and remained there on account of the First World War. A contract was signed with him to beautify the inside of the synagogue. The artists requested biblical pictures for his work, and I gave him various pictures, including Rachel's Tomb, "and it shall be at the end of days", etc. These pictures were drawn by him in oil paint on the walls. The dome was colored in the form of the sky, strewn with stars. He also drew various decorations on the Holy Ark.

The synagogue was beautiful and attractive to the eye. I did not see any like it in beauty among other synagogues that were larger than it. I enjoyed worshiping there with my father of blessed memory who sat at the east side. Reb Yehuda Szpak, may he live, sat across from him.

The Episode of Might

Despite the gray life of the Jews, various deeds of bravery took place as needed. I will tell about one of these here. Sometime in 1918, the Germans had to retreat from the conquered areas in accordance with the cease–fire agreement. Then, they wished to remove the grain from the Praboslavic Church on Rodowka Street, which the Germans had turned into a grain storehouse during the war. We found the need to oppose the removal of the grain, which we needed for our hunger. One day earlier, the members of the Bundist club came to the Zionist club that was then located in the second floor of the home of Chaim Epstein, and asked us to join together in opposing the removal of the grain and its transport to Germany, which was hungry for grain. We agreed.

The next morning, the stores, workshops and factories were closed. We gathered in the marketplace in crowds. When the German wagons laden with grain attempted to cross the marketplace on their way to Grodno Street, which led to the road to Bialystock, masses of Jews stormed the wagons. The horses were startled, and the wagons were overturned. A great tumult broke out. In any case, the German regional governor, who was supervising the removal of the grain, began to shoot. Matityahu Leisin was injured in his hand. However, this did not stop the opposition, until the captain called the German Army that was encamped in the seminary. They came with full arms and declared a state of emergency. Only then did the crowds disperse to their homes, and the Germans succeeded in their objective

[Pages 74-77]

The Synagogue Courtyard (Shul Hauf)

by Tzvi Finkelstein, Nachalat Yitzchak

Translated by Jerrold Landau

"The Synagogue Street" – this was its name from Russian times, until the Poles came and changed its name to "Berek Joselowicz Street". The Russians came once again and changed its name to "Gorki Street". We did not have time to become accustomed to the new name until the Germans came and destroyed it completely. However, the "Synagogue Courtyard" still lives in my memory, as it was etched in my brain from my childhood, and as I left it at the beginning of the 1930s. I will erect some monuments in its memory and in memory of its residents.

I will commence with the house of Kalman Epstein at the entrance to the street. He was Kalman the rope–maker. His was a stone house with a cellar below. This cellar served all of us, his neighbors, as a shelter during the time of war. In those days, the front passed through the town. The women and children slept in the cellar and the men slept in the house upstairs. The property of the Bikur Cholim society, which was lent out to anyone in need in return for a specified surety, was also found upstairs in those days.

If you went out from the house of Kalman Epstein and went to the house of Tzipa Kaplan and her sons Archik and Avrahamel, you would already be in the courtyard of the synagogue itself. As it continued on, there was the Beis Midrash, and on its left the New Beis Midrash. The Old Beis Midrash had smoke stains on it that testified to the fact that it survived the great fire that had broken out in our town before the war. The rabbi worshipped there, and prayers were conducted on all the days of the week – unlike in the other two, where prayers were only conducted on Sabbaths and Festivals – with the exception of the "Shuln Shtibel" at the entrance of the synagogue. Gemara was studied in the Old Beis Midrash in the evenings, and Ayin Yaakov and Kitzur Shulchan Aruch[1] were studied in the Shuln Shtibel.

The synagogue itself was filled with drawings. Its roof was domed, and the dome was decorated with illustrations with captions below, such as: light as a deer, brave as a lion, strong as a leopard, etc.[2] On the walls the illustrations included: a vision of the end of days, you who are burnt by fire ask about the welfare of your mourners[3], the musical instruments of the Temple, verses from the Bible and Talmud, etc. The colors were alive and bright. Legends circulated about the wonderful artist who drew all of this, and also engraved the doors of the Holy Ark with his own hands. Some people said that his own image was hidden in one of the pictures, and others said that in the dark, one could see the flames of the burning of Jerusalem as live flames. The entire community was proud of its beautiful synagogue, which was unique in the area. A cantor and a choir led services in the synagogue. On the High Holy Days, many came to hear the singing, and the crowding was great.

The new synagogue was founded and established through the efforts of Reb Shmuel Mechnik. After the death of Reb Shmuel, the gabbai (trustee) was his son–in–law Avraham Eliknicki, who was a very active Zionist activist, and one of the important men of the city. The first tribulations were taken out on this Beis Midrash. The Soviets turned it into a movie theater. It is also the only one that was not destroyed – oy, woe! All of its worshippers are no longer alive. Near the synagogue was a large wooden house in which Reb Aharon the shochet (ritual slaughterer) Leibel the carpenter, the orphans Rudy and Paltiel Lipszitz – that is Paltiel the engraver – lived next to each other. Paltiel was a wood engraver, who produced fine works. He and his son Avrahamel created all sorts of utensils and toys as souvenirs. His wife would distribute these products to rest houses far afield.

The synagogue

Next to Paltiel's house, adjacent to the New Beis Midrash, lived the widow Minia Belkin and her daughter. There was also a small grocery store in her house, the only store in the Synagogue Courtyard. Minia had another son who studied in yeshiva and came home only on occasions. (He is Rabbi Dr. Samuel Belkin, the head of Yeshiva University of New York[4].)

Izak Bordosz lived on the other side of the New Beis Midrash. He was Izak the pretzel baker. Every afternoon, Izak went around to all the houses of the town with a basket of fresh pretzels. Until today, there is no Svisloch native who does not remember the taste of Izak's tasty pretzels.

Behind the Old Beis Midrash was the communal ice cellar, where ice was stored throughout the entire summer season, particularly for medicinal purposes. A large vegetable garden stood next to it. This was the garden of Binyamin Rabinowicz, who was Niomesheine Lahs[5]. He was the only person in the town whose entire livelihood was derived solely from the growing and sale of vegetables. His neighbor was the veteran Zionist in town, Yosef Katzenelboigen and his wife Vella. They were both people of culture, and they spoke Hebrew to each other. Some said that they also spoke German. Continuing along the Synagogue Road, immediately after the Old Beis Midrash, there stood a fine wooden house, which was the house of the rabbi. Rabbi Rozen of blessed memory lived there until he immigrated to America. Rabbi Eidelberg of blessed memory lived there until he move to Makow and Plock, and Rabbi Moszkinski, may G–d avenge his blood, lived there until the Holocaust.

The last two teachers lived next to each other, next to the house of the rabbi. There was the teacher of children who was called Der Klein Rebbele[6] on account of his short height. The second one was Chaim Shlomo Szabzyn. The cheders closed down when the Hebrew School developed, but Chaim Shlomo continued teaching Torah in the school. He educated more than two generations of students, and he called each of his students with a unique nickname. Many of these nicknames stuck with his students throughout their lives. He would say to us, "Dr. Meizel was also my student, and in truth, he was not one of my better students."

Moshe Reznik lived behind the house of the rabbi. He was a simple Jew with a noble spirit. He played the violin, and also gave lessons to young people. He was the only person whom I recall playing at weddings. However, more than he knew how to play himself, he was known as someone who understood music. His advice was solicited when it came time to select a cantor. It was sufficient to look at the face of Moshke to know whether or not the cantor was succeeding.

The building of the Hebrew School stood at the edge of the road. This building formerly served as a hospital; however later a wing was added, and it was renovated, furnished, and turned into a school. Various teachers from the town and from outside taught there for some terms. One constant teacher from the beginning of the school until the end was my respected teacher Alter Goldberg. He was a modest and proper man. He attempted with all of his energy to impart to us, his students, and the values of Judaism in general and Zionism in particular. Hebrew was spoken in his home. This was the mother tongue of his children Emanuel and Hadassah. His wife Malka was an educator in the Herzliya Gymnasium prior to the world war. Behind the school was a large field. At its edge, behind a small residential house, was the slaughterhouse of the town. All of this belonged to Moshe Begun, who was also a builder and monument maker. One day Moshe Begun arose, left all of his large estate and many businesses, and made aliya to the Land of Israel as the head of his entire family.

To the left of the school was a lane that led to the fields and the river. To the right of the lane was the estate of the wealthy man of the town, Alter Mintz. There was a large courtyard that included the tanning factory and residential homes of Alter Mintz and his two sons–in–law, Minkes and Zadnowicz. Parallel to this lane was a narrow lane that led to the bathhouse. Motke the bath attendant lived on this lane. All of the wagons of the beggars who passed through the town would park in his yard. From there, the beggars spread throughout the town to collect donations. They rested there until they left for the next town.

I will describe a few other homes. Next to the synagogue, to the east of it, stood three houses. On one wide was the home of Yosef Slapak. This house was at one time the office of the communal council. On the other side was the house of Riva the fruit seller. In the middle was the home of my father, Reb David Finkelstein of blessed memory.

From the window of our house that overlooked the Street of the Synagogue, I could look at out at all of the dear Jews of our town, as they went to worship. They filled the entire Shul Hauf on Sabbaths and festivals. Children ran to school. The butchers ran to the slaughterhouse. Women carried foul to the slaughterers. Some went to the Beis Midrash, and others to the home of the rabbi. Some went to the bathhouse and others to the rivers. Was indeed all of this cut off, and is now no more?

Tzvi Finkelstein, Nachalat Yitzchak, June 8, 1959

Translator's Footnotes:

1. Ayin Yaakov is a compendium of the Aggada (story or legend type) material of the Talmud. The Kitzur Shulchan Aruch is a compendium of practical Jewish Law.
2. Similes used in Jewish law to describe how man's actions should be with respect to the service of G–d.
3. A depiction of the destroyed Jerusalem, as taken from the Tisha BeAv dirges.
4. See http://www.ou.org/about/judaism/rabbis/belkin.htm for a brief biography of Rabbi Dr. Samuel Belkin.
5. I am not sure of the meaning of this term.
6. The Small Rebbe.

[Pages 78-79]

My Grandfather Reb David Meizel
of blessed memory

by Shimon Finkelstein

Translated by Jerrold Landau

His image is etched in my imagination as he is hunched over the Gemara next to the eastern wall of the New Beis Midrash. Despite the fact that he took part in conducting his business, his main occupation was in Torah.

He was known as an expert in Talmud and Jewish legal decisions, and as a sharp scholar in the town. People would come to him to adjudicate legal questions despite the fact that he did not serve on a rabbinical seat. He was an exceptional person in the extended family of Reb Shimon Meizel of blessed memory, and honored, powerful person in the town. He was the only one who dedicated himself to Torah. He studied with the son of the Chofetz Chaim[1]. His mouth did not desist from study throughout all his days. He did not only engage in study, but also Torah research. We still have a manuscript of his whose purpose was to answer questions about Rashi through fixing the errors in the text of Rashi. He was greatly honored in the town. They waited him for the repetition of the Shmone Esrei[2], for Kol Nidre and the shofar blowing[3].

Uncaptioned. Probably the Meizel family.

He loved Zion, and enjoyed Hebrew books and newspapers. He was one of the founders of the modern Cheder, and set aside a place for it in his house. He was assisted in this by his daughter Rivka, may she live long, who now lives in Israel.

Already in 1914, he purchased a plot of land in Israel, in the village of Melel. It is still is in the possession of the family to this day, and is tended to by one of sons Shmuel Meizel, and the daughter of his old age.

Grandfather educated his children in the spirit of the love of Land of Israel and the Hebrew language. Most of them obtained Hebrew and secular knowledge. He directed all of them in the direction of aliya – and he succeeded. His daughter Rivka made aliya in 1908. She occupied herself in teaching. Later, after her sister Chaya made aliya in 1912, who studied in the Herzliya Gymnasium and completed her studies in France, they together opened a Montessori kindergarten in Haifa. His son Chaim, who excelled in his talents and was an alumnus of the Reines Yeshiva in Lida, made aliya in 1912. He completed his studies in the Turkish army. After the end of the war, he completed his engineering degree in France. He now lives in Montreal, Canada, and woks on behalf of the Hebrew language and culture.

The Community of Swislocz, Grodno District

Basha Meizel

Reb David Meizel

The third daughter Ahuva also completed her studies in the Herzliya Gymnasium. She studied medicine, and now works as a doctor in Itlit.

Grandfather made aliya in 1932. Masses of people took leave of him in the New Beis Midrash. He settled in Petach Tivka. He set a place for himself in the central Beis Midrash, and dedicated all of his time to the study of Torah. People were very content with him, and they related to him with love and reverence. He continued writing his major work there.

I will dedicate a few lines to Grandmother Batya of blessed memory. She enabled Grandfather to conduct his Torah studies and his communal work. Despite the large family of twelve children, she found time to assist Grandfather in conducting his business. She was a daughter of the fine Wolf family, who found their final resting-place on the Mount of Olives already in the 18th century.

Grandmother was very much involved in charitable works. She loved assisting her fellow with words and deeds. She died at the old age of 85 years old, and was buried near Grandfather in Petach Tivka

Written by his grandson Shimon Finkelstein.

Translator's Footnotes:

1. One of the leading rabbis of the time, who died in 1933 in his 90s.
2. The Shmone Esrei is the main component of the daily prayer services. It is recited silently at first, and then repeated out loud by the prayer leader (except for the evening service, where it is not repeated). It is customary to wait for the rabbi to conclude his silent recitation before the repetition is begun.
3. I am not sure what the reference to Kol Nidre is here – other than perhaps he might have been honored by holding one of the Torah scrolls during the service (Kol Nidre is the opening prayer of Yom Kippur). The shofar blowing here most probably refers to the shofar blowing that was conducted in the middle of the silent Shmone Esrei. Once again, it would be customary to wait for the rabbi before these shofar blasts are sounded.

[Page 80]

Shmuel Goldberg of blessed memory

by Tz. F-N

Translated by Jerrold Landau

He was a native of Krynki. He was a brother to the teacher Alter Godlberg and Chaicha the wife of Reb Efraim Berezanicki. He married a woman from Svisloch, and lived there for a period before he made aliya.

He had an alert and enthusiastic personality. During his youth, he took part in the revolutionary movement against the Czarist government in Russia. He made efforts to escape abroad. He spent time in several countries in Europe and America. He then returned to Russia, and served in the Russian army until the First World War. He was on the front, and was taken captive by the Germans. When the major Russian Revolution began, and when he saw that the Jew was the scapegoat in all of the tribulations, he gave up on the revolution and turned into an enthusiastic Zionist. He remained faithful until his last day.

He made aliya to the Land of Israel along with a group of shareholders of "Minzar", whose plan was to establish a collective factory for textiles in Jada, and to earn their livelihood from the work in the factory and an auxiliary farm.

The enterprise failed due to the difficult conditions and lack of water. The settlers dispersed. Shmuel and his family moved to live in Tel Aviv. He opened up a store on Ahad Haam Street, near the Herzliya Gymnasium. This became a meeting place for all of the natives of our town. The first news of the extermination reached him, and we conducted the first memorial for the martyrs of our town in his home.

His heart was open to everyone. His sense of humor, sharp adages, and thrilling stories filled with adventure, his intelligence and power of speech – all of these joined together and charmed the hearts of all who heard him. He was excited about every small matter that was added to the Jewish community of the Land. This enthusiasm took hold of his family as well, who were also dedicated to the Jewish community of the Land. When the members of the Jewish community were called upon to join the British army in its war against Hitler may his name be blotted out, all three of his daughters enlisted. His only son, who helped him in his business, worked day and night in the Hagana.

He merited in witnessing the founding of the state. However, he suddenly died of a heart attack during its first year. May his soul be bound in the bonds of eternal life.

Tel Aviv, May 1, 1960

[Pages 81-87]

Sislevitch In Our Generation

by Kayla Zakuta, Canada

It's already 36 years since I left my birthtown Sislevitch.

All through the years, most of them hard and painful in this new land, I never even missed the country where we were counted as strangers, oppressed, persecuted and chased.

On the other hand, my little town Sislevitch, where I was born and spent my best young years, there was left a deep impression in my heart.

No time, no distance did beat the memories, and didn't tear apart the connections of closeness and friendliness to my Lansmen all over the world.

With love and respect, and pride I always remember our little town Sislovitch. Even through the terrible hard economy and political situation the little town still progressed.

And they went farther in progress than most other towns, the close ones and even far.

Farther back in the 1900's Sislevitch had a name, "Little Warsaw".

Whether it was the look of the town, whether it was cultural and industrial development, Sislevitch still appeared a big city in miniature.

Sislevitch was one of the first towns to wake up from a deep sleep; from backwardness which it was drowned in Jewish life.

The theme of the "Enlightenment Epoch" was you should be a Jew at home and a human being outside – in Hebrew " Hiya Yahudi b' o ha lecha v' adam basatecha".

The Epoch was beating deep and put roots down in Sislevitch.

A small group of Enlighteners had a successful battle against the backward establishment of the town.

They organized the first high school, the first Chader where they taught Hebrew, the country's language and all the usual secular elementary classes.

They even started to teach in the Talmud Torah an hour a day of the country's language.

They also established a library.

The Jewish progressive parents, the ones who could spend more, of course, sent their children to high schools, which were, at that time, only in big cities.

A few of them even reached universities.

For the Jewish Holidays they, the high school students, also come with the Yisheva students to town where they parade in the streets in their uniforms with their brass buttons and ribbons.

With great respect and envy the plain (those on a lower economic level) children in the town looked at the students.

The Jewish youth in Sislevitch learned with huge enthusiasm. They read and they were making progress in all subjects.

Young Jewish men started to work in all the leather factories.

They learned professions and started to make a living and provide for themselves.

In town showed up strange people.

They were the leaders and agitators from different political parties.

Under their supervision they established different political groups.

In earnest the youth were studying and reading the now published illegal literature.

They agitated, debated, took part in secret meetings, and they often fell into the hands of the gruesome Russian Police.

The youth in Sislevitch became very revolutionary. They even organized demonstrations with red flags and songs, and went into the Police area and forced the Police to join with the demonstrators.

But right after that another force of Police followed.

They searched for and arrested the demonstrators.

One evening is engraved in my memory.

The terrible picture of a young neighbor; at our house they cut up the bed covers and pillows, they turned over the broken cabinets to look for illegal literature; the hopeless crying from children and parents when they took away their young son without guilt in handcuffs.

I was then only 7 years old.

[Page 83]

Right away the next morning I decided to go through all my books and see if they are kosher (no illegal political literature).

The first sacrifice was my Siddur (Prayer Book). I threw it in the fire in the oven. "Only the first page was missing with the script that said the way it was written was allowed by the censors."

The first sacrifice of that time was Perets Bernstein, a young boy born in Sislevitch. He was beaten to death by the barbarians in Grodna Prison.

It has to be also noted about the decisive and courageous handling by the Sislevitch youth.

In the time of the Pogrom, it spread over all of Russia, the terrible, not friendly call, Slay the Jews and save Russia (Bay Zhidov Speci Rosei) .

When the organized pogroms came close to our area, the farmers showed up in the market with axes and big jute bags ready to loot, with all the wild hate and the readiness of those farmers to go through in a wild slaughter.

Those murderers could smell that it wouldn't be an easy task. The Jewish Self Defense Youth in town were organized and decisive. They would not be killed like sheep.

I remember very well one gathering place of the Self Defenders. Part of the prepared weapons used to defend yourself were hidden in a chicken coop behind the stove in my grandpa's little apartment by the trenches.

Even though I was a little child there was still the scare and the unusual fear for that in which the whole town would have been involved was left forever in my memory.

Until today I still shake when I hear bells ringing in a church, because the ring from the church was many times a call to Pogroms.

Along with the big stream of Jews at that time a large group of the population of Sislevitch left town.

The year was 1910 when the big fire erased ž of Sislevitch. The next few years without houses, poverty and epidemics brought very hard times to our little town.

But Jews manage. Sislevitch rebuilt with nicer, roomier, and more modern houses. We didn't have time to rest from the fire before the heavy clouds of World War One came.

The years from 1914–18 were very hard ones; they were filled with pain and suffering.

The Russian mobilization, when so many young boys had to leave for the war.

And the Russian retreat of 1915.

The lootings and killings, the German invasion and the fright and danger from positions of the battlefields (the war came close from different directions).

The terrible epidemics and the long bitter suffering beneath the terrible German militaristic boots.there were years of bitter and dangerous battles for the day to day existence.

Just for a little piece of dry bread and for a garb made of old jute bags.

Life was still worse in the cultural and spiritual life of the town; all libraries, and schools were closed shut.

Every gathering and meeting was forbidden. The youth did not study anything; didn't read.

It was a real danger that the whole generation would stay backward and be demoralized.

But the Jewish spirit didn't allow the youth to be oppressed altogether.

Disregarding all the orders and danger they opened in secret Yiddish and Hebrew libraries. They taught everything until late in the night. They had to read by the light of a small flame "curnicle".

I remember how my mother used to call me the "girl with the mustache" and the mustache came from the flame of the gas lamp. The gas at that time was one of the big valuables.

Late in the night we used to wait for a newspaper or telegram which we used to pick up from the last train arriving.

Later on we could subscribe to a newspaper . We became 4 parties to the newspaper because we didn't have the few cents neither.

[Page 85]

I remember the very deep joy we had and the better mood and the expected hope which the Balfour Declaration brought.

Right away they organized the Zionist Center and right away it divided itself into different groups:

1. Ordinary Zionists
2. Rightists and Leftists, Zionist Youths
3. Rightists and Leftists, Poalei Zion
4. Left and Right, Zionist Youths
5. Bundists

6.   Peoples Party
7.   Communist

About 7–8 political parties in a town between 4–5,000 people.

And it was really very joyful and a living town. Especially after the retreat of the Germans.

I remember how in the Zionist Center we went on discussions and debates without end.

They started splitting on and on to the right and left; and when it came to elections it was in the region and the city and later on the Polish Parliament.

This little town became electrified.

I remember when I kept on and on to convince my mother she shouldn't vote like my father; she should not vote for the regular Zionists but for the Labor Ballot.

The atmosphere in the house was loaded with gun powder.

I never found out how my mother voted; she always insisted on a secret ballot.

I was sure for myself that a Labor Ballot won because of my mother's and other mother's votes.

Deep in my mind is engraved the summer of 1920: The Polish–Bolshevik War.

First the retreat of the Polish Army.

The hateful Poles, under whose Anti–Semitism the Jews had suffered so much were defeated in Sislevitch.

They hardly managed to run away in front of the Bolshevik Army's attack.

[Page 86]

What kind of fear and impatience, hope and security, did we, the Jewish Youth expect from the Bolsheviks?

I remember very well the night when the successful Bolshevik Army marched into town.

With the tune of the "Internationale (Le Marseillaise)", the wonderful speeches which they spoke in the markets, and what kind of joy and hopes we were promised in the speeches.about equality and freedom.

Oh, how naive we were.

And we believed all that.

How fast and bitter everything turned to a disappointment.

The liberation came out with a true face; drunk in their power with a funny thirst for revenge.

They ruled over the town with no restrictions.

It didn't take them long to break all of our beliefs and hopes.

We convinced ourselves very fast that the despotism and wild revenge and bloody tyranny would equality and freedom never be.

How wicked and senseless and misleading the words of the "Internationale" echoed.

We could hardly wait to be saved from this salvation.

And it became darker and darker.

For us Jews it was just like going from fire into water.

We knew very well what we could expect from the arriving Polish victors.

The wild Anti–Semites even wanted to make the Jews from the little towns the sacrificial lamb for their ugly loss and the previous retreat.

If not for the American Commission which came along with the Polish Army, the Jews from Sislevitch wouldn't have wound up so lucky.

The hard economic situation, the new orders and suppression by the Polish Anti–Semites made Jewish life not bearable to the future with no hope.

In 1923 I left Sislevitch.

I left everything which I loved so much and was dear to me.

[Page 87]

The separation was hard and painful.

I never forgot my little town; not during the week days with the hard work of making a living, and not with the peaceful, beautiful, exalted holidays from the Sabbath and the holidays.

Together with the deep muds outside Pesach Eve, and the depressed gray days before Rosh Hashana.

I also didn't forget how beautiful our little town was in the Spring when the orchards were blooming; the cornfields with the blue colored flowers from which we made wreaths.

The wonderful beautiful summer nights when the moon poured out her magic light over the big market and it looked like it (the moon) watched over the little town as it slept.

I don't want to forget the dense orchard with its dense trees; the olives always in the forest by the train where the youths used to promenade, singing, playing and having love affairs, dreamed and imagined.

There were those who also dreamed of a national home in Eretz Israel; some dreaming of a national autonomy in the Diaspora and some of a Communist Revolution.

The ideals were all different, but the dreams were all of our beautiful and bright future.

Oh what kind of dark, terrible, merciless and gruesome future it was just waiting ahead for the Jewish youth.

Young lives have been cut off in the Vyshavnyker Forest which became the mass graves of the fathers and mothers.

Burnt and erased from this earth is our little town.

Senseless did the murderous neighbors, like the wild vultures,

wait impatiently to steal the Jewish homes, belongings, and property.

Not a memory was left in that town except the Jewish Cemetery.

Now only fall winds are blowing and crying above the lonely gravestones.

Dead is my little town with all its close and dear people; but in my heart everything is alive and all their images remain.

[Pages 88-90]

My Friend Feivel Rubin
may G–d avenge his blood

by Ch. Sh. Rubin (Egosevitch)

Translated by Jerrold Landau

The poets and writers can tell us about the spiritual powers that were hidden in small towns, about the men of science and diplomacy, who were for the most part conceived and born in small towns.

Even in the most recent generation: Bialik (a native of the village of Rubche), Sokolow (a native of Wyszograd) Ahad Haam (Skvira), Peretz (a native of Zamosc), Weizmann (Motol), Friszman (Zgierz), Tshernikovsy (Mikhailovka).

All of them were born and raised in small communities. There, they received their education and their personalities were formed. The cheders, Talmud Torahs and Yeshivas forged their spirits.

We do not know what factors caused their sublime talents to take form specifically in small towns. We cannot imagine that the people of the small towns were made of better material than the people of cities and medium sized towns – in fact, the opposite is true. How can we explain why the growth and maturation of these talents, which also existed in large cities, should turn into strong trees specifically in a small town? The explanation is that there was a concentration of tradition in small towns. The love and honor of Torah was felt wherever one turned: in the home, in the house, and particularly in the Beis Midrash. A talented child was recognized, a scholar was honored, and righteousness was displayed before everybody. The spirit of Torah and the spirit of the field joined together and forged solid personalities, pining for knowledge and desirous of righteousness. The enticements to other forms of enjoyments aside from wisdom and knowledge, which were recognized and valued in the area, did not exist in the town.

In our small town as well, geniuses stood out already in their early youth. Some of them died in their prime, and other ones later joined the stream of life. Some of them did not find their way because of difficult conditions, and other ascended the stepladder.

I wish to deal with one of them here, my friend Feivel Rubin. We studied together in cheder and later in Yeshiva. It caused me no small amount of anguish that I wished to be equal to him, but I could not because of my lack of talent.

I recall that his father Eliezer Rubin first brought him to the house of my father, who was a teacher of Talmud to nine–year–old children. His father was a tanner, and he still stands before my eyes with his tanner's hands, that are not amenable to be cleaned for a long time – as he was supervising a young, eight year old child, as if he was taking care to ensure that his he would not touch the spice container with his dirty hands, as he presented the student who should learn together with children a year or two older. When father of blessed memory refused to accept him because he was too young, Eliezer stood his ground and insisted that he be given an exam. Father agreed to examine him, and was astonished at his quick grasp and depth of understanding. I followed every answer with great jealousy. Father said that this is a "vessel". He turned his gaze to me and said, "Do you see". His words were like the point of a sword to me. I nevertheless decided to measure up to him, but I was not able to. Nevertheless, I overcame my jealousy and befriended him, particularly since Feivel's home consisted of one room with a corner kitchen, and his mother suffered terribly from gallstones and spent most of her time resting with hot water bottles – despite this, the house had a pleasant atmosphere. A strand of grace was spread through every corner. The bitterness of the suffering was affected by the sweetness of the pleasure of Feivel. His mother was related to families of great rabbis, and she saw the realization of all of her dreams in her progeny. She saw me as a good friend for her son, and was pleasant to me despite her suffering. The cup of tea that his sister, the graceful Freidel, would serve to me shone with the polish of nobility. The "pedigree" and nobility instilled splendor and glory upon this home despite the poverty.

His parents ensured that he would also obtain secular knowledge. Within a brief period of time, he mastered all of the knowledge of the public school. Warchygyn's workbook on difficult math problems was simple to him[1]. Students of the Russian seminary in Svisloch would turn to him to answer their questions. However, all of these things to him were like trivial matters with respect to Gemara, which captivated him.

We were separated for a brief period, and met again at the Yeshiva of Rav Reines in Lida. This Yeshiva, which blended Torah and secular knowledge with the purpose of educating the Jewish intelligentsia in the spirit of tradition and Zionism, was not homogenous. People came to it from different strata. There were careerists who came to the yeshiva to obtain secular knowledge, with the intent of leaving later. These were cynical egoists. Others had the Zionist enthusiasm, and dedicated their studies to the learning of Hebrew language and culture in addition to the study of Gemara. Most of these people made aliya to the Land of Israel, or were Zionist activists. A third group were those who were attracted to the genius of Metich. They neglected the study of Hebrew language and secular subjects, and dedicated all of their energies to the study of Gemara, its commentaries, and didactics. Feivel belonged to that group. He was one of the choice students of the Genius of Metich. The reason for this was that he did not find a field of endeavor for his wonderful talents in Hebrew knowledge and secular studies. His diligence in didactics overtook him completely. At home and on the street, in the Beis Midrash and outside of it, one could see him concentrating on didactics. He would forget himself even when he was walking on the street, as he would wave his hands as he pondered his studies, that did not allow him to attend to his own needs. With time, political changes came that forced the genius of Metich to move his residence. Feivel also uprooted himself with him.

I separated from him and set out on a different path. I always took interest in him, and wanted to know what was going on in his life. I heard that he was swept up in the stream of life, and his talents did not spread out afar. I could not make peace with this situation of "this wonderful person being swallowed up in the earth". At the end, his fate was the same as that of his millions of brethren. He was murdered by the cruel ones.

What did these wild animals perpetrate upon our nation and mankind! How many geniuses were there, in actuality and potentiality, if a one small town could contain a few of them. Is it within our power to estimate the deep loss that the executioners inflicted upon all mankind?!

Translator's Footnote:

1.   The metaphor used here is 'like a string through halvah'.

[Pages 91-93]

Memories from my Father's House

by Yafa Szpak Rabicki

Translated by Jerrold Landau

My father Michael Rabicki of blessed memory was a native of Zwolen. My mother was Rachel Leah of blessed memory. They raised a family in Svisloch consisting of three girls and two boys.

My grandmother Chasia of blessed memory was a widow who lived with us. She was a pious and wise woman. She helped anyone in need and took part in every tribulation. I remember the situation at the time of the First World War, when the Cossacks broke into our house, which was full of women from my family and the area, in order to perpetrate pillage and rape. Grandmother took out a bag full of gold coins from her treasury and waved it before the eyes of the Cossacks. Thus did she turn their inclination toward the gold and distract them from their designs. They grabbed the gold and left.

She supported every charitable endeavor. She assisted the ill and was a faithful member of the Chevra Kadisha (burial society). She died at about the age of 90.

My father of blessed memory was considered to be well off. His hand was open to charity and the doing of good deeds. He loved Zion, donated money to the Keren Kayemet (Jewish National Fund), and read Hebrew. My mother supported the poor in her way, from within the house. Liba Dziga, one of the poor people of the town, partook of his Sabbath meals with us until the day of his death.

The education of the children was in the traditional, religious fashion in combination with secular knowledge at the level of the public school. There was no high school in our town, so we continued our studies with private tutors. Russian was the language of the secular studies until 1914. We were under German rule during the time of the First World War, and we had to study German. However, several hours were dedicated to Hebrew. The teachers were Jewish. We were imbued with the Hebrew national sprit. Our cultural activities outside of our studies were in Hebrew. I recall the play "The Sale of Joseph" that we performed successfully.

In 1918, when the Bolsheviks invaded Poland, we were under Bolshevik rule for a brief period. However, within a short period, terrifying events passed over us. When they entered the town, a command was issued that every youth must volunteer for the Red Army. Whomever would refuse would have his property confiscated and his family killed. My brother Menachem and Mendel Bigonski and Dhatzkelewicz were in a village outside the city, and did not know about what had taken place. My father, who was familiar with the Russian hatred of the Jews and remembered the pogroms, girded himself with might. He endangered his family and did not tell his sons about the command. He also convinced Leizer Chaliuta, who was in educational contact with Mendel, not to tell. The matter ended peacefully with the speedy retreat of the Russians. At the end of the war, the economic depression began in the city. Many immigrated abroad. The rest received support in the form of money and packages from their relatives. The gentiles also benefited from this. The town managed somehow, and also absorbed refugees from Lopic.

The family of Michael Rabicki

Life flowed along in an orderly fashion with the Poles joining forces with the Jews. The mayor of the town was Pawlowicki, and his deputy was Wigonski. The leadership of the firefighters was Jewish, including: Alter Broida, Menachem Rabicki, Nachum Dinowski, and others. There were many Jews in the band. In general, a Jewish atmosphere pervaded in the town. On Sabbath eves, Melech Dali of blessed memory, a pure Tzadik, announced the advent of the Sabbath. Candles were then lit in every home. On the High Holy Days, a feeling of awesome holiness was felt throughout the town. We celebrated appropriately on the festivals. The customs were observed. The joy was expressed primarily with eating and drinking, as well as assisting the needy with "Maos Chittin"[1] or in other manner. There were the traditional charitable institutions: Gemillut Chesed, Bikur Cholim, and Linat Tzedek were supported by the communal council[2].

In the meantime, the movements began to penetrate through the various strata. The youth were influenced by the movement. The organized themselves into various youth movements. Young Zion, Hechalutz Haboger, and Mishmeret Tzeira (Young Guard), of which I was a member. We stood out in our uniforms: khaki and blue ties. A counselor from Bialystock named Chavionik would come to direct us in drill practice. Our practical activities were centered on the collection of the Keren Kayemet boxes and the organization of ribbon days. We remained in constant contact with the Land of Israel. Every event there had an echo among us. The opening of the university[3] was celebrated with the lighting of candles in the houses. The day of the Balfour Declaration literally turned into a holiday. The synagogues were filled with celebrants. The veteran Zionist activist Mr. Yosef Katzenelboigen, who stood out over everybody, ascended the podium and lectured with enthusiasm. The pogroms of 1929 inspired a group of young people from Hechalutz to arm themselves with weapons. A Polish captain directed them. However, he only had time for this on the Sabbath. Rabbi Miszkinski categorically rejected this activity on the Sabbath. When it was explained to him that this was for the Land of Israel, he permitted the activity.

We also had places of Hachsharah near us, and we arranged work also for people from outside the town.

The peaceful life continued during the first years after the war. Poland was drunk with its own independence and did not afflict the Jews. The head of government was liberal. The Jews took an active part in the elections. Indeed, there were cases where gangs pillaged and murdered on the roads, and tormented bearded Jews in trains. However, in many cases, the relations between the gentile population and the Jews were very proper.

The situation changed after the 1920s. The tax burden upon the Jews was increased with the goal of removing business from them. The Polish youth began to become unruly, and searched for pretexts to begin disturbances. On one occasion, a gentile entered the store of the Jew Soloveiczik on a day of a fair. The gentile suddenly dropped dead. The gentiles became agitated, and a death pall fell upon the town. Thanks to the intercession of Jews with the keepers of law and order, and thanks to the preparations of strong young wagon drivers who stood guard, the situation passed peacefully.

The town, like the rest of the Jewish communities, became enveloped in morning after the death of Pilsudski. It was felt that the protector of the Jews departed. The Polish authorities increased their pressure upon the Jews with taxes, fees and various decrees. The entire Jewish population became impoverished. Wealthy people became needy. The Nazi spirit also spread quickly, and a general oppression pervaded the town. This feeling increased with the terrible news from the Land of Israel of the disturbances of 1936, and the white paper.

Translator's Footnotes:

1. Literally "Money for wheat" (i.e. wheat for the baking of matzo), a generic term used to describe charity given to the poor before Passover to enable them to observe the holiday appropriately.

2. Gemilut Chesed – granting of charitable support. Bikur Cholim – the visiting of the sick. Linat Tzedek – the providing of accommodations for wayfarers.
3. The Hebrew University of Jerusalem.

[Pages 94-95]

Avigdor Berezanicki
may G–d avenge his blood

by Tz. Finkelstein of Tel Aviv

Translated by Jerrold Landau

The first time I saw him was when I was a student in one of the lower grades of the Hebrew School of Svisloch during its first years of existence. One of the teachers got sick, and a young man with smiling eyes entered the class in his place and gave the Hebrew lesson. This was Avigdor Berezanicki, the oldest of the four sons of Reb Efraim Berezanicki, the owner of the tanning factory at the edge of the city at the end of Amsitiwowa Street. All of the sons helped their father in his work, and took part in Zionist activities during their free time. Avigdor, his second brother Avraham Yitzchak of blessed memory and a few other friends founded the Hechalutz chapter in Svisloch. Avigdor was the chairman of the chapter from its founding until the Holocaust. Many of the members of Hechalutz (including his two brothers Avraham Yitzchak and Yosef) made aliya. Avigdor did not succeed in this. Aliya was closed down by a decree of the Mandate authorities when he was preparing for aliya. His fate was as that of the rest of the Diaspora.

During its years of existence, Hechalutz in Svisloch conducted Zionist–pioneering cultural and educational activities. Its members eagerly participated in general Zionist activities as well. With his help and energy, a pioneering Hachsharah kibbutz was established, whose members worked in the factories and sawmills of the town. Within Hechalutz, the older Zionist youth – lacking any future in their place of residence – found a purpose and direction along the path of pioneering Hachsharah and aliya to the Land. Many of the townsfolk who studied in Hebrew educational institutions in Vilna, Grodno, Bialystock – such as Feivel Haperin, Hershel Finkelstein, Moshel Elkonicki and others – became involved in the cultural work of the chapter until they made aliya. When they left the town, Avigdor Berezanicki was the only one who continued on in the leadership of the chapter. I remember that I went to take leave of him on the eve of my aliya to the land. He walked with me from place to place in the factory that was attached to their home and said: "look at each and every detail and give over to my brothers in the Land a living picture of their father's house", as if his heart prophesied that he would never see them again. May G–d avenge his blood.

The first Hechalutz organization. Avigdor is in the center.

[Pages 96-97]

In their Memory

by Shimon Finkelstein

Our house was on Warsaw Street, which was partially populated by Jews. The civic garden was at one end of the street. There, the youth would enjoy games of sports, and weave their first dreams of love.

This street lead to the boulevards on the route to Jalowka. The boulevards were crowded with people out for a stroll on Sabbaths and festivals. The river that cut along the road served as a place for bathing, laundry, and Tashlich[1] on Rosh Hashanah. From there, the windmills could be seen about which many stories circulated. The houses of the gentiles were surrounded by fruit gardens, and the houses of the Jews were bare. Our home was large, and stood out was its closed porch and colored windowpanes. The porch served as a dwelling place for us on the holiday of Sukkot, when the shutters of the roof were opened[2]. We children decorated it.

During his youth, father was active in the first revolutionary movement of 1905. He was active with the defense when there was a fear of pogroms, and he was always a communal activist. He was a member of the local committee during the German occupation of the First World War. Later, he became a member of the communal council, and was active in the Zionist movement. He donated and canvassed for the funds, and was called upon as a mediator in monetary disputes. He was observant of tradition. On Sabbaths and festivals, particularly on the High Holy Days, a sprit of holiness pervaded the home. He donated generously to the Beis Midrash, and maintained a claim on specific honors. For example, the opening of the ark for Neila[3] was my father's right. I recall that once American guests arrived, and he gave over this honor for a high price. I felt this to be a great travesty and injustice, and I entertained the though of jumping ahead of the American to open the ark. It seems to me that this event affected my relationship with the Beis Midrash and the prayers.

The Finkelstein family

Father was also the Torah reader, and he read the Megilla[4] on Purim for the women and elderly people in our home. His business was in the manufacture of leather. There were good and bad times, and during the 1930s, he thought about liquidating his business and making aliya. However he put this off for some time. Later, aliya became difficult, and even I, who made aliya in 1936, was not able to help.

My mother of blessed memory, Pnina of the Meizel family, excelled with her great contentment. She studied Hebrew, as did all of the members of the Meizel family, and she served as a teacher in Jalowka and Sokolka during her youth. From 1911 to 1913, she studied in the course of kindergarten teaching given by Michael Halperin in Warsaw. She continued teaching Hebrew after her graduation.

There is no need to state that our parents concerned themselves with the needs of the family, and were diligent in the education of their sons and daughters – particularly mother who had received a complete Hebrew education.

I had three sisters. All of them were talented and socially oriented. Thanks to them, our house was bustling with youth and exultation. Despite all of the efforts of the parents to educate their children, the children had to forge their way in life with great effort. My eldest sister Menucha completed her studies at the teacher's seminary in Grodno. She served as a teacher in various places, finally at the Hebrew Gymnasium in Pinsk. My sister Leah studied in Slonim and build her family in Mikszewicz. My third sister Sara, who excelled in her beauty and talents, completed the Gymnasium in Slonim with excellence and was about to enter the university in Jerusalem, but she met with difficulties. During the Russian period, she served as a nurse in the hospital of Bialystock.

I remained in the land and concluded my studies at Mikve Yisrael. I awaited their aliya. This idea did not depart from me until the Holocaust came and cut down our family along with myriads of families of Russian and Polish Jewry.

Translator's Footnotes:

1. A prayer service conducted at a river bank on Rosh Hashanah, which includes a symbolic casting off of sins.
2. To make a Sukka.
3. The final service of Yom Kippur.
4. The book of Esther, which is read publicly on Purim.

[Page 98]

The Jewish Settlements near Svisloch

by Naphtali Eden

Translated by Jerrold Landau

As we erect a memorial monument for our town, we should not neglect the memory of the nearby area. There were two Jewish settlements a distance of a few kilometers from town: Alibod (Colonia Galiliska) and Mikhalka (Colina Izrailska). They were strongly connected to our town with regard to all types of communal institutions, such as the schools, synagogues, etc. They were founded approximately 200 years ago by the Russian king Alexander II, who wished to scatter some of the Jews in villages, thereby turning them into a productive element. In order to expedite this process, he freed the Jewish settlers from army service and various taxes for the first 25 years, and granted the Jewish settlers the same rights that were given to Russian farmers. At the beginning, the relationship between the Jews and their neighbors was good. They even helped them at first with the work of the land. However, during the 1880s, with the outbreak of a wave of anti–Semitism after the murder of Alexander II, the relationship took a turn for the worse. The Jews of the settlements, who were already more or less rooted in farming, and some of them even in other trades such as tailoring, shoemaking, dyeing, flour milling, postal services, etc. – began to feel that they were no longer in favor with their neighbors. At that time, Baron Hirsch, as is known, advised settlement in Argentina, with his great support. Some of the settlers moved there, others moved to nearby cities, and still others moved to the Land.

Despite the fact that several families left the settlements, the situation of those that remained worsened, for those that left sold their land to Russian farmers. Despite this, the Jews loved their settlements, and they did not want to leave their land, which was very dear to them. We estimate that there were approximately 10 families in Izrailska (Mikhalka) and several dozen families in Galiliska (Alibod).

[Page 99]

The Revenge on the Police Commissioner

by Eliahu Ayin

It was 2:00 on a nice hot day in the summer of 1907. Because of his love of music the Volunteer Fire Brigade took into its orchestra, the young boy, Srulke Zuses. They (the Fire Brigade) dressed him up like a miniature fire fighter, with ribbons, belts, and a silk robe with tassels. The boy, with pride, used to play the drums as he walked over the streets. From everywhere people used to come to the orchard which people called, "the little horses," the park with the big old maple shade trees. There walks (today) two thirds or three quarters of the Jewish people in Sislevitch, with its official name Swislocz, to give honor and an honorable good–bye to the Police Commissioner who is being transferred to the county capital of Slonim, in the same state as his superior, the Police Inspector.

He (Police Commissioner) was different than most typical Russian officers. He was a calm man, a good one, a pleasant person who hated to have unpleasant occasions. In Sislevitch there were a few hundred well paid leather workers. All were revolutionaries. He never bothered them and he let the boys play. He always said they didn't bother anybody, and when their draft (notice) will come, a part of them will leave for the military service, another part will run away to America and some of them will be free; and those who are left will come back from the service and get married. And that will be the end of the revolutionaries. After the wedding the girls will not become revolutionaries. That's why if somebody reported to him, or if an order came from Volkovisk to make a search in somebody's home, he would quietly inform someone (who would mention it to the affected person), so as to give them time to hide illegal books and proclamations.

There was also in town wet tanneries to work on the skins. The workers in the wet tanneries were mostly low paid farmers. The town people didn't want to spend time with a "stupid hobby" (they did not want to work for such small pay).

[Page 100]

In the orchard they made speeches with compliments to the Police Commissioner. The young Alcohol Tax Collector was leading the orchestra as the fire brigade played the music. Everybody sat down on the grass, ate well and drank beer. Then, in the name of the community, they presented to the guest a silver cigarette box with a fitting inscription. The honored Police Commissioner made a thank–you speech and was very moved. When the ceremony was finished he was lifted on people's shoulders and carried around while everyone was shouting "hurrah, hurrah."

The new Police Commissioner who came to replace him was also present. He was more of a spectator than a participant. He thought to himself, "What a beautiful spectacle. Everything is good and lovely, but what is the end?" The superior of the Police Commissioner knows very well about the Revolutionary Movement in town. He knows how big the Bund is, the S.S. (Territorialists), the Poali Zion. He even knows there are a few anarchists and Russian Nationalists. He knows even about the only Jewish Pe–Pe–Es'nik, which the Polish Party educated and trained to organize but did not use because they committed terror acts in the big cities in Poland. He knows there are meetings around town, discussions in the house of study, in the orchard, in the alleys of the trees, in the Warsaw streets, and in the forests of Vishnek, Patzu, and others. The Police Commissioner reigns over a large territory for a few years and does absolutely nothing at all. It is not for nothing that the Police Commissioner lost the trust of his superior. Once there came to the county office an anonymous report that 2 dangerous revolutionaries came to Sislevitch. The Superior right away sent some of the Volkovisk Police to make a search in the middle of the night without the knowledge, until the last minute, of the Police Commissioner. The two revolutionaries were watch makers. They really came to look for work, and they found jobs here. One of them had the flu which was an epidemic at that time. The searchers even checked the pieces of toilet paper. Even though

[Page 101]

they didn't find anything, the Superior still didn't trust the Police Commissioner.

" For his popularity in the community the Police Commissioner now pays a dear price. The Police Commissioner is not only for the little town but he is over the whole state which takes in a few little towns and many villages. The job of the Superior, although he is over a big city, in reality has a lower level job. A Russian officer must be very smart to protect his livelihood with might and life. The best way to be promoted to a higher rank is to be hated by the population, especially by the Jews. I will remember everything well."

And sure enough, later on, that's the way it was. The new Police Commissioner showed his dissatisfaction with the 20 Ruble monthly wages he quietly received from corruption. The Jewish Community paid him a bribe for not bothering the kosher butcher shops. He asked for more. The residents understood well that if they gave him more, he would later ask again for more. They were in no hurry to pay him. It didn't take long and he showed what he could do. And the news traveled from mouth to mouth that the Commissioner is going for "sanitary inspection." Everybody went to their garbage boxes (in their back yard) and made them as neat as possible. They swept the yards with brooms and sprinkled yellow sand on the ground, just like the floors in their homes. The Police Commissioner, together with another clerk came, and if they found a piece of paper on the ground or the garbage box didn't appeal to him, he would write up a protocol (report) and that is the way he went from house to house.

Very often you can see him late at night sneaking around behind the windows with his ears pointed to the apartments. Probably he is preparing to grab a Revolutionary. With meetings and gatherings we have to be very careful. We have to put guards very close, one next to the other. We have to improve our system of signals through whistles. The Revolutionaries came to the decision that the only thing that could help (them) was to win over the Police Commissioner. Ssshsh, I can hear a bugle. Yes, it

[Page 102]

is the bugle.There is a fire somewhere. I take a look out the window and I see very close–by a fire. I think it is Mosha Yahuda, the tailor's house. I run outside and I can feel that Mendel Isaac Pinhas is enjoying and getting a lot of pleasure blowing the bugle, and very loud. It is about an hour after dinner. Outside there is mud, and it is wet and slippery. Everybody is running to Amstibover Street and enjoying doing a mitzvah and yelling out "fire." We can soon see them coming with the barrels of water on wheels or a pump on wheels, and we put up our hands and help them get to the fire. Still further, where the gate to close the city over night against enemies is located, close to the School for Christian Boys from town and close villages, burned an old barn. On a wet evening like that, from what and how it happened nobody knows.

Everybody who helped put out the fire was proud of himself. But who can compare to the Russian who held the water hose in his hands. He was so shaky and worried somebody would take it away from him. He listened to me, a young, schnook like I am, what I told him. I told him "I read somewhere that a wide stream of water from a hose puts out the fire better than a solid stream." I yelled at him,

"Spread it." Right away he put his hand on the opening of the hose and spread around the water.

The barn was torn apart into pieces and the fire was as good as out. The crowd was getting smaller and smaller. Sometimes we could hear a creak from one end of the ruins and then an answer from the other end.

It was a tradition, and maybe also a law for many years that the Police Commissioner must come to take a look at the scene of the fire. The next morning I heard the news; when the Police Commissioner went back (home) from the fire, some strong, agile

person sneaked behind him with a rock in his hand and gave him (the Police Commissioner) a blow to his head. And now the Police Commissioner is bed–ridden and we don't know if he is going to survive. He laid there for many weeks.

[Page 103]

When he recovered he became a good man, a soft one. So good "you could put him on an open sore (very literal Yiddish translation)."

And Sislevitch became very lucky to have the best Police Commissioner they ever had. They told me that before he left they gave him a bigger good–bye party than the previous Police Commissioner. Years later I was told that the hero (boy) who did the town such a good dead was Moshka Potsoher.

Firemen in Action

[Page 105]

Oh, My Small Village!
(in memorial of my village Svisloch)

Devorah Eden

Translated by Asher Szmulewicz

Eh, my small village!
The cradle of my life, of my home!
Only remains are left,
Like a few leaves of a beautiful tree.

I remember your market, the big one,
Your houses are measured by beauty and

charm,
In the middle – a pole, white and tall,
With a shining cupola, like a golden crown.

On the streets, on the alleys moved along,
From all the corners and from where
The life swarmed,
Shining and blossoming children and youth.

Shabbat – disappeared years and uproar,
The Holy Spirit hovered there;
Yet knowing the Torah and the
Enlightenment
The youth dreamed and aspired.

And just the synagogue courtyard, an
intellectual corner
A house of study with Torah scholars and a
synagogue;
Day and night learning, replenishing,
Shabbat and Holidays full of prayers.

And Slichot at dawn, hitting the shutters,
A voice was heard like a divine echo;
"Jews, wake up for the Slichot!"
And immediately to the synagogues they
came.

[Page 106]

Shabbat and Holidays eve,
Calm and joy were felt around
In the streets, the alleys and the orchards
The joyful youth used to walk.

The faces were illuminated and shining,
And songs were ringing in the air.
With spirit and holiness, with enchantment
Each house and each alley were fragrant

Everything disappeared in great pains,
Suddenly from a murderous hand,

The Community of Swislocz, Grodno District

With nothing left, no witness
Except for the stones, and the silent wall.

Only the earth and the trees from the forest
From their mass grave,
From our relatives and cherished ones,
Have heard their last cry of pain.

Cry of despair, supplications
With calls of mercy and to God
Only the murderers answered
With a diabolic laugh and mockery.

Your remnants, without news from you
Being far from you scattered
In your awful sufferings,
Nobody with a tear went along with you.

Not the years, the storms will wipe out
From memory presently the horror and the dread,

[Page 107]

That the paintbrush cannot paint
And the mouth cannot describe.

But your remembrance, our relatives,
We will carry you on our silent heart,
Like a holy memorial, it will be in front of our
eyes
And go along with us everywhere

The Community of Swislocz, Grodno District

**Dinah and Pesia Eden of blessed memory around the
tombstone of Moshe Dov Eden of blessed memory**

[Pages 108-111]

The Destruction of Svisloch

by A. Ayin

Translated by Jerrold Landau

According to the article of A. Ayin in the Yizkor book of Volkovisk, according to the testimony of: Simcha Kaplan, Emanuel Goldberg, Meir Galperin, Avraham Stopszowski, Berl Orlanski, Yerachmiel Lipszitz – partisan, and according to the testimony of two Christians from Svisloch.

In September 1939, German airplanes bombed the military train in the Svisloch train station, and a large number of Polish soldiers were killed. After a short time, the Red Army conquered the town.

A civic committee was established under their rule. The leather factory was confiscated, and a director from outside was appointed. Similarly, the best houses were confiscated for the use of outside officials. These included the houses of the rabbi, Leizer Chaliota, Minkes, and others. Religious study was forbidden, and the cheders were closed. Life slowly got established, and the residents began to become accustomed to the new authorities.

The Germans attacked the town from the air in June 1941. They spread leaflets stating that they had come to free the world of Jews, and that their property would be confiscated for the benefit of the Christians. Many set out to flee to Russia, but the routes were already blocked. The Nazis conquered the town on June 26, 1941. On the first day of the occupation, an edict was issued ordering all of the Jews to register and to wear a white band on their left arm. A few days later, the Jews were ordered to wear a 10 cm yellow patch on the left side of the chest and a second patch on the back of the right shoulder.

Many young Jews were shot during those days under the pretext that they were Communists. Heavy fines of money and goods were imposed on the Jews, with terms of a few hours for payment. The penalty for non–payment would be immediate shooting. There were Christians who collaborated with the Nazis. Many of them turned into Nazi followers, and snatched Jewish homes and businesses.

In accordance with an edict of the Nazis, a council was formed, headed by Szlachter, the principal of the Hebrew school, and assisted by Efraim Zadnowicz. The other members of the council were Mendel Wigonski, Alter Borda, Motka Kalmanowicz. The secretaries were Dr. B. Meizel and Pinia Kleinerman. All edicts were sent to this council, and it was responsible for carrying them out. In July 1941, a ghetto was established through an edict of the Nazis. It included the area of the synagogue courtyard and Grodno Street. The Jews were commanded to move to the ghetto on that day, and to bring their horses and livestock to the market to give over to the Christians. Life in the ghetto became hell. The murderers would break in to the ghetto, beat the Jews and steal whatever they wanted. The Jews were forced to work at all sorts of difficult, degrading tasks under the constant guard of Nazi gendarmes. Announcements were posted on the streets forbidding Christians under pain of death to sell anything to the Jews, particularly food. Nevertheless, an underground commerce opened up between the Jews and the Christians.

In the spring of 1942, Commander Adenbach summoned the head of the council and commanded him to gather together all of the Jews between the ages of 15 and 60, men and women, to send them to work on the road that had been paved between Baranovitch and Bialystok. The edict was filled immediately. The Jews of Svisloch worked on the section that was next to the village of Kvatery. They worked for 12 hours consecutively, with meager food. Nevertheless, they worked diligently under the false hope that this would save them from death. Despite this, the Nazis found reasons to beat many workers over the head with rubber clubs. When the Jews asked for help from the council, the request would be turned to the commander and the officials, who would accept bribes for whatever they still had. The beatings would then stop for a short period, and would then start again with greater strength, in order to extort from the Jews the rest of their clothing and money. Thus were the Jews tortured throughout the summer of 1942. The work was completed at the end of October 1942, and the Jews returned to Svisloch.

On Saturday, October 30, 1942, the Christians were ordered to prepare 500 wagons. The rumor spread that this was to expel the Jews from the town.

At dawn on November 2, the Germany army and Ukrainian, White Russian and Polish gendarmes surrounded the town. On Monday, November 2, 1942 (Cheshvan 22, 5702), at 5:00 a.m. they began to expel the Jews from their homes, including the elderly and infirm. All of them were commanded to gather in the marketplace. They were permitted to take only their personal clothes. The gathering area was in the destroyed stores between Amstiwowa and Radawka streets. The marketplace was sealed off. The Christians were commanded to watch the spectacle. At 8:00 a.m. Commander Adenbach came as the head of the German captains and began to sort the Jews: the youths and middle aged people in one place, the elderly and infirm together, and the women and children together. The group of youths was arranged into rows of four and marched to the train station via Brisk Street. Many people whose bags were too heavy to carry left their bags aside, and the Christians snatched them. At the train station, they were loaded onto transport wagons, 80 in a wagon, and sent out in the direction of Volkovisk. A few remained outside due to a shortage of space on the wagons. Those were gathered together, sent out to the Wyszbinik Forest and shot. The elderly, women and children were led along Rodowka Street and Hauf Gasse to the Wyszbinik Forest. Those who fell behind were loaded onto wagons, including the rabbi of the town, Rabbi Chaim Yaakov Miszkinski, his wife, and other town notables.

Pits had been prepared in the forest. The victims were commanded to strip down to their underwear. They were lined up in rows of ten, led to the pits, and shot. According to the testimony of Simcha Kaplan, the rabbi lectured to them to encourage them in the Sanctification of the Divine Name[1]. They did not shoot the small children, but rather tossed them into the pit alive. Some were beaten over the head with clubs. (As told over by a Christian). Some of the Jews were appointed to bury the quivering bodies. They were promised that they would be left to live. The forest was surrounded with a heavy guard to ensure that nobody would escape. This murder aktion lasted all day. Toward the evening, when they realized that the slaughter had not yet finished, the rest were lined up in rows and shot. All of them, including those lightly injured, were cast into the pits. After the conclusion of the slaughter, the murderers went up to a villa in the forest and celebrated all night. The Jews who were involved in the burial were imprisoned in the cellar of the villa. They too were shot the next day. According to the testimony of Avraham Stowaszewski, several succeeded in escaping from the villa. However, they made an error. Rather then running in the direction of the Bilibizh Forest, they ran in the direction of the Biritowicz station, where they were captured and murdered.

The belongings of the Jews were gathered up by the Germans and brought to a grain storehouse. The best were sent to Germany and the rest were sold or distributed to the local Hitlerists.

The youths were brought to Volkovisk, and put up in six bunkers (for their fate, see the next article). Out of a population of 3,500 Jews of Svisloch, only four remained alive: Meir Galperin escaped to Bialystok, and was sent from there to a work camp; Berl Orlanski escaped from the camp in Volkovisk and succeeded in joining up with the partisans. Niame Lewin was tortured in the Auschwitz and Dachau camps until she was liberated by the American army; Yerachmiel Lipszitz escaped to Bialystok and also succeeded in joining the partisans. One girl, Alta Szeweliwicz (the daughter of Yossel Broszka) also was in Auschwitz until the liberation. Then, she came back to see her native city, and was murdered by Polish murderers who recognized her as a Jewess. Aside from those, 38 Jews who were living in the region during the Nazi occupation survived. Some of them were by chance in different places at the time of the conquest of the city, others escaped from the camps and joined the partisans, and still others served in the Red Army or were sent to Siberia at the time of the Russian conquest of the city.

The children of Pinchas Alichowicz

Translator's Footnote:

1. A textual footnote appear here, at the bottom of page 110: "Simcha Kaplan was not among them. He heard these things from Christians, when he went to visit Svisloch after the war."

[Pages 112-114]

The Torture that the Svisloch Natives Endured in the Volkovisk Ghetto

by the Editor

The information given here is what I gleaned from the booklet on Volkovisk published by "YIVO Bletter", which mentions the martyrs of the area including the martyrs of Svisloch, and other testimonies.

All of the Jews 40 years old and older (according to the words of Mrs. Winkelstein), were concentrated in a narrow ghetto, consisting of the synagogue courtyard and the new alley. The younger people were expelled to a prison in Volkovisk. The number of deportees was at first shrunk by the murder of 10% of them. This was done by arbitrary selection or a "game" by the Germans. Dr. Noach Kaplinski relates in the booklet on Volkovisk, page 20: "The commissar made a game in Svisloch. From among the Jews who stood in queues to be deported, he removed 200, and arbitrarily shot every tenth one on the spot."

When, and in what condition did the deportees arrive at the prison – we can read in the words of Hershel Rotman, page 20, on November 2, 1942: All of the Jews of Volkovisk had to gather by 10:00 next to the barracks. When all of the Volkovisk residents were gathered, camps of Jews began to arrive from the entire region. By Tuesday evening, all of the Jews of Zelva, Porozovo, Amstiwow, Pisk, Mosty, Svisloch, Ruzhany, Liskova, and Izabelin had already gathered. They came tattered, beaten, and weary. They all walked on foot. In exceptional circumstances, the children were brought on wagons.

The "Events" in the Bunkers

There were 20,000 people in the bunkers, consisting of two blocks (fifteen bunkers) of Volkovisk. A bunker was designated for about 500 people. Six bunkers were for Svisloch. In accordance with this calculation, there were 3,000 prisoners from Svisloch[1]. From where would there be such a large number of Jews below the age of 40 in Svisloch – for it is impossible to believe that they would have let the Jews of Svisloch live spaciously without filling up the bunkers. It is clear that what is written above regarding the transport of 200 was only one of the transports. Other places in the booklet also imply that the number of Svisloch Jews in this prison was large. The fact that the Jews of Svisloch, along with the Jews of Volkovisk and Ruzhany were left for the last implies that the deportation to the death camps was in inverse proportion to the number of Jews in each community.

They started with the smaller communities and ended with the larger ones. The community of Svisloch was one of the last.

It would seem that in the most recent period, refugees came to Svisloch, which was a city of manufacturing and industry. Perhaps as well the small communities in the neighborhood of Svisloch were numbered along with Svisloch.

The Torture in the Bunkers

I will not tell about the torture of the Jews of Svisloch separately. Since the fate of all of them was the same, it is sufficient to discuss the fate of the martyrs in general before they were sent to the death camps. We will bring only two sections of what is stated there: "The hunger grew stronger. When it was heard that a transport of potatoes arrived at the camp, the starving Jews fell upon the wagons, for everyone wanted to assure himself of a few potatoes. Immediately, shots were heard. These were the shots of the German guard into the crowd due to the "disruption of order". Several people died and were wounded. However, the hunger was greater than the fear of the gun. This scenario was repeated several times a day. The hunger dictated that people would risk their lives for a few frozen potatoes (page 43).

In another place, a delousing of a group of 70 people from bunker number 3 is described. "Late one evening, when the bunker prisoners were already sleeping except for those ones, plates of sulfur were ignited. The doors were closed with the 70 people inside. Only the unfortunate people knew what went on in the bunker that night. We got an idea of what went on the next day when we saw as the doors of the bunker were opened. The bunker was saturated with the odor of sulfur (sulfur dioxide). The vast majority of the victims lay dead in various states of contortion and convulsion. The horrible torture was etched upon their faces. Others were still snorting with their last energy. One girl was groaning almost inaudibly, "Water, water". One young person with amputated legs lay with his face in the plate. His head was down and his legless body was stretched upward. Apparently, he wished to quench the burning sulfur with his body. Thus did 70 Jews die in terrible agony by a gas that would have barely been able to kill insects and lice through a duration of 12 hours."

The rest were deported to the camps of Auschwitz and Treblinka. They were not deported all at once, but rather in transports. The Jews of Svisloch and Volkovisk were in the final transport, perhaps because these were the largest communities. By December 20, only 5,000 of the 20,000 Jews that were in the camp remained. These were mainly Jews of Volkovisk and Svisloch (page 21).

Here is not the place to review the spiritual and physical torture in the death camps, for much has already been written about this, and the fate of the Jews of

Svisloch was certainly no different than the fate of their millions of companions. The annihilation was complete, with the exception of a few remnants, a portion of who were later killed. We will quote what was written there (page 34) about the survivors. Hershel Rotman writes: "From the Volkovisk transport, Yosef Kotlirski and Niame Lewin of Svisloch came with me to Dachau. They survived."

"From the people of the Volkovisk camp, only a few girls remained, including Alta Szeweliwicz." Her fate is described in the preceding article.

Translator's Footnote:

1. There appears to be an error here. If there were 20,000 gathered, and 500 people per bunker, there would be 40 bunkers rather than 15.

The daughters of Dina Drachinska–Eden of blessed memory

[Page 115]

The Testimony of Mrs. Winkelstein

I was already not in the town at the time of its annihilation. I fled to Minsk in 1941, and from there I wandered to various places in Russia.

I girded myself to return to Svisloch after the war. I arrived in the town via Baranovitch and Slonim.

The Jewish city was completely burnt, except for Savcza Olica (The Street of the Dogs) – the place of the tanneries. The remnants of the government were found in the rest of the houses. In the town, I found a lone Jew, Leibel Edelsztejn, who had also returned from wandering. My situation was extremely difficult. I was in constant fear, for the Jew hatred peered forth from the wrathful eyes of every gentile.

They looked at me as a madwoman. They were surprised that a Jewish soul had remained. I slept at the home of a gentile by the name of Distnik who in his day had been poor. Now, all good things were found in his home: furniture, blankets, dishes – all from the booty.

From the gentiles, I heard about the Holocaust that had passed through the town. At first (they did not know dates) they enumerated the Jews by age and sex. The young women were placed separately, and the men separately. According to the gentiles, they were sent to Malkin (Treblinka). The rest were concentrated together in the synagogue courtyard and its near environs (the ghetto). Three families were placed in each house. They were permitted to conduct business and to work. Apparently, the Svisloch hide manufacturing continued on. Their situation was relatively good, which misled them to believe that they would not be afflicted.

The gentiles told about the annihilation. All of the remaining people between the ages of 40–60 were gathered up. They were told to take suitcases. The entire camp, headed by Rabbi Miszkinski and the Shamash Melech, was brought to the Wyszbinik Forest. The gentiles (Poles and Russians) had prepared a large grave there beforehand. They stripped their clothes, sent them into the pit, and buried them alive. The grave – as was related – pulsated for some time (The person relating this sighed at this point.)

I saw a tablet with a Magen David upon the grave, upon which was inscribed "The Jews of Svisloch". I do not know who erected this marker.

[Pages 116-117]

From the Letter of Yerachmiel,
a Svisloch Partisan

Germany, October 8, 1947.

Hello to you Moshe, and all who ask about me, many greetings!

Forgive me for my poor Hebrew. Of course, this is due to the seven years that I did not use the language at all. On the contrary I attempted to "uproot it". This was the tendency in Russia. Are you interested in the matter of Naftali?

"I let Naftali in 1941, during the days of the Germans. In the Svisloch Ghetto, we were often together for many hours, and we always talked about you fortunate people. Naftali worked as the assistant to the secretary of the Judenrat, Pinia Kleinerman. This work exempted him from the backbreaking work of the accursed Nazis. I saw your father often. On numerous occasions, he even worked at the backbreaking work together with the rest of the Jews, but from the time he became the "honorable chairman of the Judenrat", he was completely exempted from the forced labor of the Nazis. On the terrible day of the aktion, your mother and father were the first to fall in sanctification of the Jewish name. Afterward, all the rest of the elders and important people of the city were murdered. Naftali ended up in the young people's camp, and became part of the Volkovisk Concentration Camp. Your brother escaped from there along with Yaakov Golombowicz, Yerachmiel Wytnik, Tzvi Kapusta and several other youths from the Svisloch region. As Tzvi Kapusta told me, a disagreement broke out between the fleeing youths. Yaakov Golombowicz said that one of the farmers should be paid to guard their souls from the Nazis until the end of the war. Yaakov had enough money. I do not remember the opinion of Naftali. Yerachmiel Wytnik said that that proper route was to obtain weapons and join the partisans. As I was told, your brother and Yaakov did not support this idea, and therefore the members rose up against Yaakov and extorted his money. Downtrodden and beaten, your brother took him, and they returned to the Volkovisk camp. However, the Nazi guards murdered them before they arrived.

Favar Szlachter the director told me about their murder and deaths. He is also not alive. With regard to the story of the rest of the group, I examined the matter carefully, and found that Kapusta's story was correct.

I will tell you in brief about the events of my life. I lived in Svisloch until the outbreak of the war with the Nazis. I worked for sometime at forced labor. When I was still in Svisloch, I became convinced that only the partisans had found a proper means of revenge, so I joined them. Slowly at first, and later in the open, I went out against the Nazis. Despite the announcement that I issued and my calls to those that were prepared to do so to come out to the forest, the people of my town did not listen to me. Thus, the members of my family were also murdered, despite the fact that they knew that they had a forest, and that I was in the forest. I grieve and have no comfort over this. I found comfort in the Bialystok Ghetto. I entered it to publish an announcement. I found an echo to my voice. A strong partisan group, consisting mainly of Jews, was set up under my direction in the forests of Kryniki and Jalowka. Most of them are still alive. Many of those who excelled remained in Russia, but I with my "tokens" and five letters of thanks from Stalin that I received for my excellence in battle – I brought with me here. The main thing was faith. I did not weep about my fate; my eyes no longer shed tears. I went straight to life; I left the fortunes of Russia even though I was a devoted Communist in Russia. I became engaged to a woman, and now I have a wife and a son. I have one comfort, which is the knowledge that hundreds of Nazis and Germans fell at my hands. I exacted revenge for the book of my family, and I did not allow the honor of our nation to be desecrated.

The Families of Moshe Rubin and Shmaryahu Margolis who perished in the war, and the Shay family

I visited Svisloch last year, and I found letters from survivors. I got them in touch with their relatives through Ayin in America, and I also found comfort from that.

I saw Svisloch, the communal grave, the destroyed cemetery, and the gravestones that to this day are wallowing in the floors, streets and yards. I saw the bitter situation and fled from there straight into the future.

I wish you a year of your own liberty and freedom

Yerachmiel

[Pages 118-129]

I am the Woman who Witnessed Tribulation[1]
(From a letter to Avraham Ayin in the United States.)

by Gittel Slapak–Shechter

Translated by Jerrold Landau

When the war broke out, I lived in the town of Svisloch in the Grodno region. My parents Kalman and Liba Slapak, their unmarried daughters Reizel and Rachel, my brother Leibel Slapak and his wife Beilka (nee Zaltzman), the parents of two year old Rivka, all lived there. Three of my father's brothers and their families also lived there.

I, my husband Boris Ceitlin and our four month old baby lived next to my parents. We all worked together with Father in his sawmill, and earned a comfortable living.

The Second World War broke out on September 12, 1939, and Poland fell within a few weeks. The Germans and Russians partitioned Poland. In this partition, our town fell in the Russian section. The Russians immediately began to execute their plans. Obviously, we were not pleased by them. They destroyed our typewriters and telephones. Early one morning, armed soldiers came to us as father was standing, reciting his prayers. They told him to stop his prayers, for he had "prayed enough". They imprisoned him, but they sent him home the same day. However, there was no end to the tribulations. They came each night to requisition flour – specifically at night as if to vex us.

After a short time, the keys to the enterprise were taken to us. It was confiscated, and we were not even allowed to walk over our threshold. The situation worsened from day to day. We were afraid of exile to Siberia. Therefore, we decided to move to Vilna, my husband's hometown and the place where many of our family lived, in order to disperse ourselves among them and free ourselves from the tribulations that fell upon business owners.

We packed up a few of our household belongings and moved to Vilna to live with my father–in–law. My husband found work in a government enterprise, and we were not lacking in anything.

The Nazis attacked Russia in June 1941. They conquered eastern Poland, including the city of Vilna. Then the tribulations began. A dizzying set of edicts were issued each day: the yellow badge, the ban on walking on the sidewalk, the ban on purchasing in stores. On Sunday, they would get drunk, beat Jews and pillages their houses. On the other days of the week they would snatch up men for work, as it were. In truth, they imprisoned them in the Likishki Prison. When the jail became full, they would bring them to the Fanar forests surrounding Vilna and murder them. In this manner, they murdered thousands of men who were snatched up in the yards and the houses. After a short period, they decided to concentrate the Jew in a ghetto. How did they make the ghetto? They falsely accused the Jews of shooting at the Germans. As a punishment, they killed many of the Jews who lived in the Jewish center of Vilna, and then they brought into the ghetto all of the Jews who lived in the rest of Vilna. We, who did no live in the center of Vilna, were brought to the ghetto with the rest of the Jews on the Sabbath Day. The Lithuanian police carried out the expulsion. They went into the houses. People were permitted to take only as many clothes as they could carry. Then they were expelled into the direction of the ghetto. Obviously, they attempted to take large packages, but in the tiring journey, walking without rest, they abandoned most of their belongings, which became booty for the gentiles. They were prodded along the way, and my 2 ¼ year old child walked on foot in fear from Vilkomirska to Starashona – a journey of several kilometers.

At first, two ghettos were set up. These were not sufficient for all of the Jews. The first people went into the houses, were they slept adjacent to each other at night. The rest remained in the yards – also crowded. From the window, I could see people standing crowded together as salted fish in a jar. This situation also did not go on for long. That night, the "homeless" people were removed and brought the place where they were brought. In this manner, "space" was made in the Vilna Ghetto.

The rest were registered by the Jewish council that was appointed in order to maintain contact with the German authorities and to execute their edicts. Aside from this, there was also a Jewish police force.

Life in the ghetto was particularly difficult, with crowding, lack of food, and fear of death. A portion of the ghetto residents worked in the ghetto institutions (hospital, children's homes, council, police, etc). Another portion was called out to work in organized groups, in accordance with the needs of the Germans. Each group was led by several leaders, who led them to an unknown place. It was forbidden to walk alone. I left my child in the children's home, and went out to work in the gardens. My husband worked in brick manufacturing. I was happy with my work, with the thought that I would be able to bring a bit of food to the ghetto, where there were no stores, no distribution of food, and which was cut off from the outside world. There was extra protection over the men, and my husband was not able to bring anything. However, the women brought some food to the houses, despite the ban. They would gather some vegetables, hide them in discrete places, and bring them into the ghetto. Or they would sell haberdashery to the gentiles, and obtain some food in return. The gentiles did not obey the ban on selling to the Jews, for they wished to make a profit. Toward evening, they would hide it in their sleeves or dresses, with their hearts trembling with fear. Black haired women such as I would plod along slowly to the ghetto. We would be frisked at the entrance to the ghetto, and if they found something, the guards would steal it and administer beatings.

In the meantime, the Germans began to execute their plan for annihilation. One night, they decreed that everyone had to gather next to the ghetto gate and to register their work certificates. Everyone ran to the gate. The murderers opened the gates and brought out a group – a quota to be murdered. These did not return. All were murdered. They would exchange certificates every two weeks, and at every exchange, they would carry out an aktion of murder. The number of residents of the ghetto continued to shrink. There were not enough certificates for everyone. Those who did not receive certificates were sentenced to death at the next aktion. When the yellow certificates were being issued, my family did not get one. I do not recall the dates, but I remember that this was in the first few months of our living in the ghetto. After the yellow certificates were issued, they summoned the certificate holders to the ghetto police. This took the entire night. The "game" began early the next morning. Those who would conduct the murder aktion were standing near the gate. Those who held the yellow certificates stood in a line and went out the gate. They were very exacting, and examined each certificate. I took my child on my shoulders and stood in the line of the holders of yellow certificates, for I had nothing to lose, and even a German could make a mistake. At first I did not succeed, and the German thrust me back into the ghetto. I was desperate. I said to myself: death is better than a life of torture and fear of death. I wished to enter to the group of those designated for death, but my husband insisted that I try again, for perhaps I would succeed in saving the child. The second time, I succeeded and left the ghetto. All of those who went out were sent to places of work, but I had nowhere to go since I did not have a certificate. Out of fear, nobody wanted to join me to their work group. I began to walk randomly through the streets. The first street was Zvolne. I walked outside all day with my child in my arms, alternating between napping and crying, apparently from hunger and thirst. I asked a Christian girl who was standing on the sidewalk to buy a few apples for me. She refused. She only fulfilled my request after great urging. In pain and agony, I somehow went through the day. I had nowhere to turn when it got dark, and I became desperate. I attempted to return to the ghetto. I saw hundreds of guards next to the gate waiting for the command to enter the ghetto and gather up all of those who did not have the yellow certificate. When I saw this, I returned and went to my Christian neighbor. Nobody saw me. My neighbors received me in a friendly manner, even though there was a death threat upon them if I would be found in their home. They served me food and gave me a clean bed. I did not eat or drink all night. The next morning, the Christian neighbor went to ascertain the situation, and to find out if I could return to the ghetto. He told me that all night, Jews were dragged from the ghetto. Those who had yellow certificates remained in their places of work, and their families returned to the ghetto. At the gate the guard asked me where my husband was. When I answered that he was at work, he let me in. My husband told me how he was saved from being killed. A large group hid in the cellar. The guards found them, but they accepted a bribe and left them. When those left, other guards came, and took what whatever those poor people had left. When there was nothing left to take, they too, sent them all to be killed, including my husband. At that moment, a merciful nurse passed by, who knew my husband, and had a yellow certificate. She said that this was her husband. There were not personal certificates in the ghetto. Thus my husband was saved that time.

We were in a very bad situation. We could not go out to work. We had no food, and there were rumors of a new aktion in the near future. We were not the only ones in this situation. The only alternatives were suicide or flight from the ghetto. In 1941, there were still places of relative quiet. We planned our flight from this ghetto. We got in touch with a yekke[2] – an army man – who would take us to Oshmyana (White Russia), a city near Vilna. The mass murders did not begin in White Russian until 1942. He told us that he would be waiting for us at 6:00 a.m. on Sadova Street next to the ghetto. But how would we succeed in getting out of the ghetto that was surrounded by guards. We got up at 2:00 a.m., and looked for some opening, but could not find one. Every gate was filled with people who were in our situation, who were also searching for a means of salvation. Between 5:00 and 6:00 a.m., when the gate was opened for the first group of workers, many broke out of the ghetto, including us. The guard of the gate could not control all of them. We did not take out any bags in order not to arouse suspicion.

After we left the Vilna Ghetto, the small ghetto had already been liquidated, and there were only about 3,000 families left in the large ghetto. These were families that possessed the yellow certificates. The German told us to enter a large truck covered with a tarpaulin. He received his money, and took us. We reached Oshmyana, first to the German guard and then to the ghetto. We arrived in Oshmyana in September 1941 and remained there until March 1943. The Jewish community of Oshmyana received the first refugees pleasantly. They provide them with housing and other material aid. That week, the guard changed, and refugees were no longer allowed into the ghetto. They shot them all. Despite this, during the first weeks, refugees streamed toward Oshmyana every day, but none of them succeeded in entering the ghetto. There were heavy guards on the roads. The refugees were caught and murdered. People were taken from the ghetto to dig pits and bury the dead.

We lived with great crowding there. There were two families in one small room. The physical situation was particularly difficult. We were called out to work every day, and food was not distributed. We would take clothes off from our bodies and exchange them with the gentiles for coarse flour and potatoes. Even the child did not taste any sugar. Jews were taken out and murdered on several occasions during our time in the ghetto. The murder aktions were carried out primarily against old people. All the people of the ghetto were commanded to gather in one place, young and old. They were taken to a place outside the city and killed with shots. At first, the plan was to murder the women and children whose husbands and fathers had previously been murdered. However, as a result of negotiations, the Germans agreed to murder the aged rather than the women and children. A death pall fell upon the Jews in the ghetto on account of the rumors that arrived from White Russia, that Jewish communities were being liquidated one by one.

Suddenly, the Germans changed the boundaries in such a way that Oshmyana was severed from White Russia and annexed to Lithuania, which was already judenrein since 1941, except for a few people in the ghettoes of Vilna and Kovno. In March 1943, the Germans informed us that they were liquidating the ghetto in Oshmyana and transferring all of the Jews to Vilna or Kovno, in accordance with the desire of each person. Confusion arose. The people had already lost their faith some time ago, but there was choice, one had to decide. Some registered for Kovno. We, natives of Vilna, registered for Vilna. The authorities ordered wagons from the Christians to transport us. Later we found out that all of those who registered for Vilna arrived in peace, but those who registered for Kovno were shot in Fanar.

In March 1943, we arrived back at our first ghetto, and the hell began anew. Once again there were registrations and work permits, and 8 people were put up in a small room. I went back to my former work in the gardens. The living conditions in the Vilna Ghetto were as described previously. In July 1943, rumors arrived about new murder aktions, and in August, we awaited the impending disaster. According to the rumors, this time, people were not taken out be murdered from the ghettos, but rather from the places of work. Signs of this were that the smaller work places where only tens of people worked were cancelled, and everyone was concentrated into two large work camps: the train station and the Provnak – the airfield that was 7 kilometers from the city. Approximately 2,000 people worked in the two work places. I was designated for Provnak. I went on the first days. Pits were dug all day. I did not go on the second day. When I went to sleep at night, the

Jewish police arrived, took me out of bed, and brought me to the police station of the ghetto, where I sat all night. (This is what the police did if someone did not show up for work, the next day, they were forced to go.) I was not the only one. The next day, a representative of the Jewish council appeared and told us that we do not have to be afraid of the "aktions". The rumors were false, and should not be afraid of going to work. That day, they did not force us to go to work. They told us to go home and eat, and whomever wishes should go to work. I believed the representative of the council. The proof was that he did not use force. I ran home, had a bite, and took my child to the children's house. This time he hugged me strongly, cried, and did not want to stay in the children's house. I went with the hope of finding some food for the family. Women wept on the way to work. Armed Lithuanian and Latvian gentiles walked on the streets. The women did not stop wailing. They said through their weeping that we are "guests" in the world.

When we arrived at Provnak, they closed the gate. Armed Germans dug around the fence. Wailing broke out at this sight. Some people began to jump over the fence. The guards started shootings, and some were injured. The shots stopped when people stopped fleeing. Then the commander of the Jewish council arrived (his name was Gennis). He calmed us and promised us that we were being brought to work. Having no choice, we believed him. Transport wagons were ready there. We were loaded like animals, and the doors were closed. The windows were covered with wire. We traveled for three days and three nights. Food and water were not distributed. We finally arrived in to the Vaivara camp in Estonia. We had left Vilna on August 6. The camp was surrounded by a wire fence, and there was a guard day and night.

There were bunks in the camp for sleeping, with three levels, bottom, middle and third. 70–80 women were in one room. There were two camps, one for men and one for women, with a wire fence between them. The director of the camp was an S. S. man called Shenbel. He arranged role call, selected staff (heads, secretaries, kitchen, laundry, bath). Most of my neighbors in this camp were divided into various work groups. I worked in paving roads, the railway or the forest. About a month later, a second transport was sent from Vilna to Estonia – these were the families of the first transport, including my husband and child. The children had their own block. It was possible to see them after work.

We were woken up for work between the hours of 3 and 4. We were given a bit of black coffee and lined up for role call. We would stand for hours until the camp commander appeared. We would stand in the heavy rain, and the rain would penetrate to the flesh. Then they would drill the men with useless exercises (during the role call, the men and women stood in the same place, and the children were supervised in the bunks): taking of the hat, putting it back on, and the action had to be done at one time. If someone did not succeed, he would be beaten until he bled. After these tortures, we went to work under the supervision of the guards.

We would work under the command of taskmasters all days, and suffer harsh blows. In the evening, we would return under guard to the camp. There would be another role call. Supper was coarse bread and thin soup. Then we would go the bunks and the beds.

There were groups that worked among civilians. If, out of hunger, someone asked for a piece of bread in a house or from a passerby, the supervisor would write down the number. (In the camp, we were not designated by patches, but rather by numbers on the arms or chest.) At night, this information was given over to the camp director. Then, the role call would last for hours. This person would be beaten. For this purpose there was a special table in which the head and legs of the person would be placed. He would then be beaten on the back with thick sticks until they were broken. The screams of these beaten people would ascend to the heavens.

There was no water in the Vaivara Camp. They would bring water in cars for cooking, however there was no water for washing. We had no change of clothing, for we were snatched up for work when we only had our work clothes. Therefore, we became infected with lice within a short period of time, and a typhus epidemic broke out as a result. Then the camp was declared closed. We did not go out for work. I was among the sick. No special care was given to the sick, no medicine or any special food. As time went on, the weak ones died, and only the strong remained alive. I do not know for how long I was ill. When I regained consciousness, I examined my body, and it was putrefied. Lice swarmed on my body, and I could not sleep at night. Once, they brought me water and let me wash myself. Clothing was also distributed. The women looked like animals, emaciated, without hair. Pills were distributed in the food that shut down the menses, so tat the women did not have any period from August 6 1943 until the liberation on March 10, 1945.

We remained in Vaivara until January 1944. Then, the camp was liquidated. Those ill with typhus and the children were sent on a train to an unknown location. My husband and child were among them. They were then lost to me forever. Those who had become healthy went on foot. The stronger held up the weaker so that they would not stumble along the way, for those that stumbled were shot in front of everyone.

I walked in the deep cold for the entire day. Toward evening, 150 men and 150 women remained in the Jevi camp. The rest continued on.

I was in Jevi for two months. I worked in the station in the cleaning of snowy railway tracks. Later, the Jevi camp was closed, and they brought us to Ereda. There, I worked at backbreaking labor. All day long I worked in Thon in the building of bunkers. The living conditions were equivalent in all of those camps. In all of them, the supervisors were members of the S. S., who were appointed for that with one objective. Except for Vaivara, there was warm water, baths, and separate camps for women. The Ereda camp was closed around August 1944. Then, the Germans were already suffering great losses. The Russians were advancing. They wished to transfer us to Germany. The camp commander counted us. I did not stand up straight during the role call. The commander lashed out at me and beat me on the head with a wooden stick, to the point where I was dripping with blood all over. After the role call, we were loaded up onto transport wagons and brought to Reval[3] to be loaded upon ships. To our dismay, there was no ship for us, so they marched us on foot for a few hours to a field, where we camped out for several weeks. On the first night, we slept out in the open. Later, they brought boards, stuck them together into shelters as if for dogs. 10 – 12 people slept in such a shelter. We were brought back to Reval a few weeks later. That day, Jews from the various camps in Estonia arrived in Reval. We were all loaded onto transport ships. We arrived in Danzig, after three consecutive of days of travel without a piece of bread or a sip of water. There, we were loaded onto small boats. It was so crowded that it was impossible to sit, so we crowded together standing. We were certain that they would take us to the depths of the sea to drown us. However, we reached land in the morning. After walking some distance on foot, we arrived at a large concentration camp called Stutthof. This was true hell. We were not taken to work, but rather tortured randomly. First, they sent us to bathe. Before entering the bath, the "doctor" examined us to see if we had any gold or precious stone. (The gold and furs were already taken from us in 1941.) After that, the SS. woman shouted at us to open our mouths, so she could check if we had anything under our tongues. She also checked under our arms. We washed up. Simple, torn clothes were distributed. We were cold in those clothes, so we did not hurry to go out early in the morning for role call. Then the S. S. women attached hoses to the taps and poured cold water upon us so that we would run to role call. We stood at role call for several hours despite the cold. Then everyone was distributed a slice of bread – the food for the day. We were not allowed to enter the bunk, so we sat outside all day. There was another role call at noon. After that, we were given some foul water upon which was floating some vegetable or a piece of beet. We ate the solid part with our hands, and we drank the liquid from the bowl. There was sand beneath the bowl. Sometimes, there were some leftovers after the distribution. This would be distributed. Sometimes, women struggled for the leftovers, but the distributors hit them over the head with the mixing spoons until blood came from their heads. One woman was left with a wound in the shape of a spoon on her forehead, which was dripping blood. There was another role call in the evening that lasted for hours (3 role calls a day). Once, as I was trembling from cold at the time of the role call, I placed my hands under my arms to warm them. Immediately, the S. S. rained blows upon me.

A selection took place in Stutthof every day. A large number of army men appeared, and all of the women had to pass by them as naked as on the day of their birth.

The army men would check them appropriately. If a wound or blemish were found on someone, they would be separated to be brought to be burnt. I passed through several selections. From there, transports were sent to hard labor. They chose the young ones and those with strong muscles. I also was sent with a group of 300 women. We were sent to the Roshin camp near Danzig. Before we went, we were taken to the bath, and clothing was distributed. Each person received a shirt, a pair of underwear, a dress, a coat, a kerchief for the head, a pair of socks and a pair of clogs. They told us that they had dressed us for two years. The appearance of this camp was like that of the rest of the camps, fenced with wire, and carefully guarded. There were blocks of bunks with hard beds, and a warm bath. The 300 women were divided into groups for hard physical labor. Some of them changed railway posts, a very difficult task. Two women were required to prepare six posts a day. They had to loosen the screws, remove the stones from around the posts so that we could remove them, replace them with new posts, screw them in, and strengthen them with filler stones. A train passed by in the evening to check if the work was done properly – that there were no vibrations as the train moved.

Another group worked in building, in the loading and unloading of bricks and cement. They had to prepare the building materials. I worked in building. This work was easier than the railway work. Another benefit was that British prisoners worked at this task, and they would receive packages from the Red Cross. The prisoners would send us a little bit of food and letters of support every day, encouraging us that our suffering would not last much longer. This eased our suffering. Ten women worked at this place. An S. S. woman guarded us. The work director was an elderly German from the simple folk. He would serve as a go–between between us and the British. He distributed the packages in such a manner that the S. S. woman would not notice. The women who worked in changing the posts fell like flies. Already having been previously tortured, and with inadequate food, they could not carry out the work. The supervisor would list the weak ones, and every two weeks they would be sent to Stutthof. Some strong ones were also sent.

In the meantime, the months of December 1944 and January 1945 approached – the months of cold. Since we were wearing light clothes, we tried to wrap ourselves with think blankets beneath the dresses, which was forbidden. When the S. S. women detected this, she imposed a collective punishment onto the entire camp. That day, no food was distributed in the camp. There were many such days. Later, they sent us coats. My coat was a Hassidic kapote. Then, a typhus epidemic broke out in Stutthof, and it was impossible to send out the women to work on the posts. Then the building women were sent to work on the posts. I worked in the Danzig station (Langfrau). I felt my energy dwindling day by day. One day, two of us had to collect the iron grates. My partner had no strength, so we only carried a small amount of iron. The S. S. woman noticed this, and slapped us both over the face, without paying attention to the civilians in the station. After a short time, I stopped working, for I had no more energy to screw crews, and my feet would no longer carry me.

In the meantime, the Russian front approached, and they transferred us from this place. We walked on foot the entire day. We slept in a barn at night. Thus did we walk from village to village. In the morning, they would distribute a dish made out of potato peels at the place we encamped. That was all for the day.

Thus did we travel for two weeks. We finally camped at a small camp near a village. We did not work. However, we almost had nothing to eat except for a small piece of bread for two days. If we stood near the fence, sometimes a piece of bread would be tossed at us. However, the camp director and the S. S. women did not permit us to stand near the fences. Once, a piece of bread was thrown to me over the fence. People realized this, and the starving women gathered around me, fell upon me, tore off my kapote, pushed me to the ground, and wanted to take the piece of bread by force. I struggled with them, and during the wrestling, the piece of bread broke apart, so neither they nor I had it. We nevertheless remained friendly, because this was only due to hunger.

We went to sleep as usual on March 9, 1945. They woke us up at night and commanded us to continue walking. A heavy guard watched over us, made up more of policemen than women. The road was full of army people and weapons. We thought that they would shortly shoot us. They brought us into a barn. We slept. In the morning we saw women – not from among us – sleeping. Some of them were ill with typhus. They told us that they had been resting in this manner for six weeks, and some of them had died. A terrifying scene was standing before us. Later, the head of our camp came to comfort us, telling us that we would not remain there on account of the filth and illness. Since we were clean and healthy, he promised that we would continue along our way in the morning after breakfast. Two hours passed. Suddenly we realized that our guards had disappeared. We looked around. The roads were full of tanks, including Russian ones. This was on March 10, and it was near the city of Lenburg. We were confounded at this sight. We did not rejoice, for we were certain that after what we had seen over the past few months, with the streets covered with corpses (these were people who died along the way), what would be the chances of finding our families? Very slim. Nevertheless, we did not remain in the barn. We went to the village. The Russians gave us food and drink.

We remained in Germany for a month without doing anything. After that we, a group of women from Poland, set out toward Poland. We arrived in Warsaw on May 1. We registered with the central committee. They gave us addresses of ruined houses where we would be able to sleep on the floor. Thus it was. We slept on the floor. We ate the leftovers of what we had brought from Germany and searched for family. I traveled to Bialystok a few times hoping that I would meet someone. To my dismay, Svisloch was within the borders of Russia and Bialystok was within the borders of Poland, so it was difficult to get to Svisloch. I returned to Warsaw. They advised me to work at a Jewish children's shelter in Otwock. I received work. At first, they did not receive satisfactory effort from me. I was lacking in strength. They had a proper director, Bilicka Blum, whose husband had fallen in the Warsaw Ghetto. She and her two children were saved, as they disguised themselves as Aryans. She realized my situation, and ordered me to eat and drink in order to first regain my strength. That is what I did. I regained my health, and worked there until August 1946. I could not longer live in Poland, since I saw the Jewish destruction at every footstep. I decided to travel to Israel and to live among Jews. I put a bag on my back, stole over the Polish–Czech border, and later over the Austrian border. I arrived at Bad Reichnhall in Germany. Incidentally, when I was in Otwock, I wrote to the magistrate in Svisloch to ask about my family. I received and answer that my parents had been killed in the Vishvinik Factory, and my sisters were sent to Volkovisk, and from there to Treblinka or Auschwitz with the rest of them. In Germany, I traveled to Berchtesgaden, Hitler's residence. I enjoyed looking at the ruins, with a feeling of revenge. There was no remnant of the evil den.

Bami Serlin

**Yafa Drancinska
of blessed memory**

Translator's Footnotes:

1. This title is a paraphrasing of Lamentations 3:1.
2. Generally a term for a German Jew. Here it seems to imply a German gentile who was friendly to the Jews. It is seemingly someone who was willing to help the Jews – obviously for a price.
3. A camp near the capital of Tallinn.

[Page 130]

Svisloch

by F. Lis, Argentina

Translated by Asher Szmulewicz

Edited by Erica S. Goldman-Brodie

The Yahrzeit of the Svisloch victims falls on Cheshvan 22. They were pulled out of their houses and dragged to the market place, sorted to death. Part of them later were dragged to the Wishenik forest to be killed; there the children were thrown alive in a mass grave. The remaining people were sent to Wolkowisk and from there to the gas chamber of Treblinka, Auschwitz, in the crematorium, where they were burnt to ashes.

I can see all of them alive in front of my eyes, when I left Svisloch one year before the war, when you could feel the breath of Hitler and the Polish antisemitic fascists. I see from my small street Berik Jaslewitsh walking back from work at the Jewish tannery. I see, from my window across the street, the Hebrew school "Tarbut" where 300 children learned. They used to run happily in the street whenever there was a recess. I always used to look at them and thought: what will these children do when they finish the school? The Poles do not let the Jews to do anything. I see the old and weak music teacher Goldberg with lung problems, a Zionist. He always used to come to me and say silently: I wish that in the new world the 5-year plan will succeed, it will be good for the Jews and for the entire world, and a flare of hope illuminated his pensive eyes. I see the Chumash teacher, Chaim Shlomo, an old man with a grey beard. He had another work, every Friday, to give "raffle tickets" to poor people for Shabbat meals. His word was holy for all the house owners in town. I see Motke the bathhouse attendant opening a large empty stable to house the poor people who used to come

[Page 131]

on a half-covered cart together with grandchildren. Motke did not charge them. I see them going to the old house of study across the synagogue. In the morning all the three sextons used to bring a Jew who was missing for the quorum (minyan). Across the street lives the Rabbi. He came out. I approached him to help me to fill the documents needed for my son to emigrate to Argentina. He did it for me willingly and said: "He should travel in good health, here things are not going well". I see Melech the synagogue sexton, the whole week in the tannery, on Friday evening running fast all over the streets and the alleys, the laps of his long coat opened with his haughty beard, his illuminated eyes, shouting under all the Jewish windows:" Women, it's time to light the Shabbat candles". I see the children of the Jewish Weltlicher school and count, six classes with four teachers for whom there was never enough money to pay next year. I see the drama. Gathering by the synagogue, the Yiddish evening classes, the box events, the theater who used to light the town with songs. I see the synagogue management divide itself and going to demand the member fees of 10 groschen a month. The teachers, the children, the youth and the administration were full of hope of a better tomorrow. I see the big market place where the Jews were selling various goods, around the market shops, in the middle booths between the goods, several terracotta pots and other similar items. And for all this you had to pay taxes, the bailiff often used to take out everything from the home, up to the last stool. I see the young people standing at the market intersection and their only thought was: emigration at any price. I see the butchers standing with a sullen face when Madam Frister passed the law through the Polish parliament against the Jewish ritual slaughter. From sixteen butcher shops, only six remained. I see Avraham Laiser standing in the market tall like an oak

[Page 132]

surrounding young people so the gentiles were frightened to assault the Jews which was a usual phenomenon during the latter time in Poland. I see my neighbors in a market day going to borrow a few zlotys in order to buy something. They are all living in my memory, but no one is really living.

[Pages 132-134]

My Wanderings
(From a letter to Avraham Ayin on March 20, 1958)

by Moshe Rubin

Translated by Jerrold Landau

… I lived in Svisloch before the war, and I owned a tannery in partnership with Mendel Wiganski (Mendel–Pesile's). I was married and a father of children. My parents, three brothers and three sisters also lived in this town. They were all married, and all of them had families. Einstein, the husband of my youngest sister, was sent to Siberia by the Bolsheviks. He survived and lives in Tel Aviv. All of the rest perished.

I was in Svisloch during the Nazi invasion of Poland. Svisloch fell into the hands of the Bolsheviks. They nationalized my factory and appointed me as technical supervisor. I remained in this position for a few months. I was then fired, despite the fact that I was needed by them as a professional. They did this in order to demonstrate to the workers that they were distancing the owner from his factory. After that, I obtained a position as an accounting director in Volkovisk. From there, I was transferred to Pisk, and from there finally to the estate of Borisovchizna near Luna, in the division of military aviation.

The Nazis bombarded us at dawn on June 22, 1941. The son of Shlomka Michaelkers of Svisloch worked as a barber in this division. The civilians fled to the fields when they bombarded the airport. During this, I met the aforementioned. As I was talking to him, I expressed my opinion that if the Bolsheviks would be defeated, it would be appropriate to accompany them on their retreat to Russia. His answer was, "You do not know the Bolsheviks, I am afraid of them".

The army announced to us that every citizen is permitted to retreat with the Russians. I agreed to this, and the son of Shlomka remained there.

Thus, I traveled with the Russians. We suffered difficulties along the way, for the Germans pursued us. Nevertheless, we succeeded in breaking through the way. I worked in the division that served the frontal aviation as a citizen. I was a storekeeper in the army kitchen. This situation continued until August, 1941.

After that, they drafted me and sent me to the brigade that was camped in the field near Moscow. After the brigade completed its formation, it was sent to the front. Our brigade acted as a veterinary clinic about 50 kilometers behind the front. We would administer first aid to the horses, and afterward send them to be decapitated.[1]

The Germans advanced quickly, and the front came within a few kilometers of us within several days. To my good fortune, I did not fall into the hands of the Germans with my brigade, for before that, I was sent (on October 3, 1941) along with five other soldiers to accompany several wagonloads of injured horses to the hospital in Tula. I was not able to return to the brigade, for it had been captured by the enemy.

They then began to arrange new formations from the remnants of the captured brigades. During the months of October and November, 1941, I was in a brigade that stood behind Moscow. Finally, I was enlisted in a brigade of several hundred soldiers who came from regions that had formerly been part of Poland and of Germans that were Soviet citizens. All of these were considered as inappropriate to serve on the front. All of us were sent to a work group in Siberia. The trip took about a month. We reached Shadrinsk in the region of Sversdlovsk. The cold was particularly harsh. We were transferred a distance of 100 kilometers into the forest on winter wagons. Bunks were prepared for us there. After two days, our division was sent to cut down trees in the forest. I and a few others were assigned as accountants in the office.

We had very difficult times in Siberia. We half starved in the first year. Afterward, our condition improved slightly until the salvation arrived at the end of the war. We were then permitted to return to Poland. On March 13, 1946, I left the village where I had lived for 4 ¼ years. There was no means of transportation. I set out on foot to the station at Shadrinsk in the harsh cold (a distance of 100 kilometers). From there, on March 18, I joined a group that was gong to Poland. On April 15, the eve of Passover, the group arrived to Chozhov (in the region of Kharkov). At the station, I heard that there was a possibility of joining up with a kibbutz, which would enable me to make aliya to the Land. I submitted a request, and was accepted t the kibbutz of "Hanoar Hatzioni".

That night, we conducted a lovely Seder. For the previous several years, I was unable to do so. I did not even know when the holiday of Passover was.

I tarried a few months in Poland. I set out with the group on July 1946. We crossed the border to Germany in an illegal manner. We were delayed in the British Zone, and we only arrived at the American Zone at the beginning of October, 1946.

I worked as the secretary of "Hanoar Hatzioni" in Munich, Germany. I lived in Rotshveiga near Munich. This was an estate where Jewish youths trained in agricultural work. There I met my wife, who had spent the war in a camp in Czechoslovakia, and was liberated by the Russians.

In Germany I received help from America, sent by the generous activist Avraham Ayin, who searched for the survivors of our town and provided them with the necessary aid. I will never forget the material help and spiritual encouragement that we received in those days.

We arrived in Israel on October 10. My wife and I obtained work in an educational institution.

We are satisfied as Israeli citizens. Our desire is that we will not be disturbed in the development of our small country.

Moshe Rubin

The Community of Swislocz, Grodno District

Sara Ayin (in Canada), Moshe Rubin (in Israel), Yehuda Serlin and Anshel Anchins who perished

Translator's Footnote:

1. This sentence is not worded very well. I expect it means that they administered first aid to some horses, and killed other ones.

[Pages 135-139]

From a Letter

by Yacov Panter

February 6, 1958

Dear friend, Ayin,

I was enjoying very much reading your answer. It was also a big joy to read such a good Yiddish. I am ready to answer you herewith, on your questions.

You asked me what was my job as an announcer. In the DP camps, there were two committees. One was from the survivors and the other one was from the "UNRA", that means the American authorities. Because we did not have any Jewish print available right after the war, a department was created to be able to read the news to the camp's people aloud through a microphone. With the permission of the UNRA we told the people news from the world and also news from the camp. We had an editor whose responsibility was to the UNRA.

You must understand the kind of situation we were in right after the war. Some of our people were just not like normal people yet after the Holocaust. On some people the camps left psychological marks more than on others. I have to admit that right after liberation none of us was normal 100% at liberation time – if you let a man out of a cage where he was starving, was dirty like an animal and let him free from slavery.

We wound up being free and not so free. We found ourselves living in camps originally built for the German army and where German soldiers lived until the last minute. The camp was fenced around with one gate for coming and leaving, guarded by an American patrol. This was not yet full freedom. I can remember once I decided to leave the camp and go down–town. I asked for permission. They wouldn't give it to me and not explaining to me why not. Once I decided to climb over the fence where the fence is low. While climbing, I heard some shots. The guards were shooting. I could have been easily killed by a bullet after liberation, just for wanting to be on the other side of the fence. There is quite a bit to tell of how the liberators behaved to us after liberation. The liberators worried that we should not encounter German people. They complained that the Jews take their milk and butter away.

Herewith I am writing you answers on your questions; I lived in Warsaw with my family, my wife, of blessed memory and my dear two little girls, one girl age 6, and the other 2 years old. The picture of my family when the Germans separated us is always before my eyes. I was together with my family just until 1941. The first day of the Hebrew month of Av when Germany attacked Poland, Warsaw would not surrender and the fighting lasted a few more weeks. We could feel already the smell of the barbarians but also hoped impatiently for an end to the fighting. On top of the bomb–raids, there was also a big shortage of food supplies. For a drink of water we had to reach the Vistula River. Hell for us Jews began as soon as the Germans occupied Warsaw. We also had to take care of the Jews from the surrounding small towns. We also had many refugees from the big city of Lodz to take care of. From all directions, people were eager to come to Warsaw. All the sufferings we went through is hard to write down on a piece of paper. We have the German atrocities and bad treatment by our own Polish gentiles.

A short time after the occupation we could move around freely but not for long. The murderers organized and started a Ghetto. The Ghetto had been surrounded with a brick wall in a small part of the old Jewish neighborhood. Any Jew found outside the Ghetto walls was shot on the spot. The problem of starvation, epidemics and death was spreading fast. This went on until the day of Lamentation in the year 1941. One morning on a Wednesday, Poles showed up on the streets telling us that all Jews from Warsaw would be transported to the East. Nobody did understand the meaning of it, but next day train loads packed with Jews left Warsaw for Treblinka and other Gas–chambers. One thing we knew: that the transport did not go too far since next day the same cars with their numbers came back to Warsaw for another load.

My wife was taken away on the 8th day of the action, while I was sitting in a shop and working for the Germans. My working permit allowed me to say good bye to my wife and children at "Umshlag–Plats." That was the name of the place where from Jews were sent to their death in the Gas chambers. This is the way I continued my life in Warsaw for a year longer before the Ghetto uprising. At the time of the uprising I was hiding with another 60 people in a small room on the 6th floor. When the Germans found out about the hiding place, they set fire to the whole building. With big effort, we were able to escape with our life through the roof, but we were all caught. Half of us were shot right away and the rest of us were driven to the Umschlag–Platz and from there to the death camp in Budzen, Poland. In Budzen I stayed for one year. The war front came closer and closer. We had to take apart what we built, an airplane factory. After that, they sent us to Lublin to work in an ammunition factory. In Lublin, we wouldn't stay for long because the murderers had to retreat west. Unexpectedly, one morning they pushed us into railroad cars and transported us into Germany. We have no idea where we were going. For a time we were going from one camp to another all around Dachau. We worked hard as slave labor. Every day we had victims who died, up to the day the Americans liberated us, May 1st 1945. We were an contingent of 3000 people. The plan was to get us somewhere farther. We had no idea where to. We were sure they would finish us off. We counted the minutes before liberation. My family was no different than the rest the Jewish people.

I tried to begin to get in touch with survivors of my extended family. I remembered my sister's address in Canada. Through a Jewish serviceman in the American army I let my sister know that I'm one who survived from my whole family. There was also another way my sister found out that I survived. After the liberation, the Americans put us survivors in a camp. Landsberg, was its name close to Munich. Once came through that camp the Jewish brigade, which was organized in then Palestine. In the Brigade was a man who was my sister's son, Yacov Golner. While he was sitting on his tank and waving to us, he recognized me in the crowd. You can imagine our joy. He stayed with me only one day. This was the second way to inform my sister that I survived the war. Also you my dear friend Ayin, I won't forget you as long as I live. The joy I had when I received a package from you. At that time the feeling that somebody in the world is concerned about me is not describable, this I will never forget.

In Landsberg I stayed about 2 years until my family did everything for me to be able to immigrate to Canada. I married here and settled here and made a nice living, but was never happy. The memories of my past gave me no peace of mind.

I always see my family before my eyes, and there is not a minute passing by without seeing them.

This is a short story of my past adventures. I would write a lot more, but my nerves and patience are in the way.

Be well, and regards to your family. Your friend, Yacov Panter.

[Page 140]

Avraham Ayin of blessed memory

by the Editor

Translated by Jerrold Landau

As we were editing the book, we received the sad news of the death of Avraham Ayin, after many years of disability.

The heart that beat throughout the years in the fullest sense has stopped. He would answer the call of any of the natives of our city, from all sides. The mind cannot imagine the full tapestry of interwoven lost threads during the era of the rescue. His heart and mind were all that were left in the years following his paralysis. These stood for him in his difficult struggle to find the far–flung people and to offer them support, compassion, and assistance in living.

His arena of endeavor was among the circles of the natives of our town. He did not seek fame despite his expertise in expression.

The generosity of his heart flowed from the wellspring of the most fundamental and natural love. His feelings grew from roots that were not spread out wide, but were of utmost depth in their place of growth. His family, relatives and childhood friends, who shared their breath in the pure, aromatic atmosphere of the shady forests, together gathered the sounds of the song of depression and weeping. They together heard the stories of the mighty ones of Israel from ancient Biblical times, and joined them together in the chain of holy martyrs who were murdered in Sanctification of the Name of G–d.

**The activist Avraham Ayin
of blessed memory**

Why not the breadths and far off places? In his town he found the actualization of the good and fine, the strength of spirit and fine traits, of willful effort, of Torah and Jewish wisdom, of yearnings and longing for redemption, of sacrifice and mutual assistance, and finally of the Jewish tragedy of the "lamb brought to slaughter". His small town was a microcosm of the entire Diaspora. If you look into it through a magnifying glass, you see the entire Diaspora, with all of its shadows and lights – the straightforward Jewish soul, in its pride and oppression.

Through poverty and want, without stamps for letters, he forged connections with Holocaust survivors. He not only brought them encouragement, but also actual assistance.

His soul was the most noble of the souls of the righteous, afflicted generation that were oppressed with persecutions, with paralyzed limbs, as if to further express the sublimity of the soul, the nobility, and the strength of spirit that overcomes the flesh.

May his memory be etched in this modest corner of the Yizkor book of our beloved town, and may his deeds serve as an example for his generation and for future generations.

[Page 141]

12 Year Relief Work

Avraham Ayin

In the summer of 1941 when the Nazi's attacked Russia, I was already 7 years sick. I was sitting at my house, spending my time reading, listening to the radio, and keeping busy with my family. Because I was sitting so much in the house and didn't go anywhere, contact with my landsmen was broken off. From time to time some men or women would come to visit me. Even in 1939 when my shtetl was occupied by the Russians I was still in touch with my hometown. But in June of 1941 when the shtetl was occupied by the Germans my connection with the town was torn apart completely. In the summer of 1942, my niece, Fegel Karasik, Yochke's daughter, sent a telegram and paid for a return answer and asked what happened to our family. The answer was that everybody is alive. From then on we didn't receive any more news. We did not know what to think about it. The news from the newspapers was terrible. According to the news we assumed that Hitler wanted physically to annihilate the Jews and that we are helpless to do anything about it. That's the way it went up until the year 1944 when the Russian Army broke the German Eastern Front and started to move forward to the West. Then a piece of hope was awakened in us, and maybe it is not yet too late. When I wrote my work, Sislevitch, for the YIVO I wrote in my forward that I hope that the murderer's hand would be too short to annihilate everything and everybody, and soon Jewish life will flourish again in my hometown. But, unfortunately, my hope did not materialize. From around 3,500 Jewish souls which lived in Svisloch when the Nazi's occupied the town, there were 4 left (as you will see in the continuation of my writing).

In the summer of '44 when the Russian Army took Minsk and after that Baranovitch, I took interest in the war fronts and looked in the newspapers for the war maps and hope started to grow in my heart.

I see in the war map from the "Times" newspaper that Slonim was also taken by the Russians. A day later Volkovisk was taken by them. A few days later I can see that Sislevitch was taken by the Russians and that the Russian Army is going forward to Biolystock. I was happy and I thought that now maybe I will be

[Page 142]

able to make contact with my hometown, and when the Russian Army stood already by the Vistula and by the gates of Warsaw I decided that now is the time to write, and I wrote the first letter to my family. A few months went by and I didn't receive any answer. I wrote a Russian letter to the address of the Gorodskai Committee and asked them about my family. I wrote them that if they are not around anymore, they should give the letter to any other Jew in town. I begged (in the letter) them to write to me about what happened to my family and to all the Jews in town. I wrote a letter to the same committee in Volkovisk that they should write to me any information they had on the Sislevitcher Jews. No answer did I receive. I was desperate. It was before Passover 1945. I decided to look for other means to get news about my hometown.

I wrote a letter to Russia to a relative of mine for which I had an old address and hoped that maybe I will get an answer. But until now my letters were just like a voice in the desert, but now my hopes came were fulfilled. I received an answer that she, my relative, met a partisan woman who together with the Russian Army had marched through Sislevitch. She told me that all the Sislevitcher Jews were led away to Volkovisk or Bialyostok, and there are no more Jews in Sislevitch. From the newspapers I know there is a Jewish Committee in Biolystock. I wrote a letter to them and asked if they knew anything about Sislevitcher Jews. At that same time I also wrote a letter to my relative in Russia. I sent her the address of a Christian acquaintance in the next village, about 1 mile from Sislevitch. I begged her to write to that Christian, who was a close acquaintance of mine, to see if he knew anything about the Sislevitcher Jews and my family.

From the Biolystocker Jewish Committee I received an answer that there were no Jews from Sislevitch in Biolystok; and if any survivers would come, they would let me know. A short time thereafter I received a second letter from my relative in Russia. It was the first sad news from my hometown. She wrote that she had turned to the Christian whose address I had given her, and he answered her in the following way: "Sunday, November 1, 1942, the Nazis gave orders to the Christians and all the surrounding villages that they must provide the Nazis with 200 horses and carriages to take out all the Jews from the town. When the Christian man received the order he came to my younger sister in town to say good-bye to her. When he got there she was crying and she said that 'life is disgusting. The Jews from Slonim were killed already. Let them kill us already. We can't live this way'. She also asked him to promise her that if he survives the war he would let me (Ain) and my brother in America know the Yartzeit of our mother, who had just died two weeks before the order came. My sister Chashka brought her to be buried according to the Jewish burial traditions. The next morning, November 2, 1942, all the Jews were driven out from their homes and brought to the Horse Market. There they were sorted out. Old men and women and small children separate, and all the young and middle aged people separate. The middle aged and young were taken away to the Railway Station, packed in cattle cars and sent away to Volkovisk and Biolystok. What happened to them I don't know, because until now no one came back. The old men and women and children were put up on the horse buggys and led away to the nearest forest, Vishnek. There deep graves were ready for them. Everybody was ordered to undress until their underwear. They were led closer to the graves and shot. Little children they killed with wooden poles." The Gentile wrote to me in Russian: "D'yeti obevalee derevyanemee kotshalkey" (a detailed description of what happened in the forest I have given to the Volkaviska Yizkar Book first published and edited by Dr. Mosha Einhorn in New York, in 1949).

The news from the Christian acquaintance was for me a terrible blow; I understood that no one is left from my family. I therefore decided to look for and help other Jews from my town who survived in every way I could. I worked out a systematic plan. First I contacted organizations like the HIAS, Joint Distribution, Jewish Labor Committee, Etc., so that they would let me know when they will get some news about the Sislevitcher Jews. On the other hand I began to look for contacts

[Page 144]

with the Sislevitch Lansmen in America and Canada. That was not too hard because in 1937 a society of the Lansmen started up in New York on the initative of the Lansmen Jacob and Brocha Elkin, Reverend Yosif Kapelush and his son Avrehmle Kaufman. The Society was named "Freind Fun Sislevitch", and it was active until World War II. The Secretary of the Society was Abraham Kaufman. He used to come and visit me from time to time, and he provided me with the names and addresses of some lansmen.

And third I started to read long lists of surviving Jews in the Yiddish newspapers. I wrote letters to the Jewish Committees in Warsaw and Lodz; and all that work didn't give me any results. My wife and friends were making fun of me. "Who are you looking for? They are all dead." But I was stubborn and never gave up the labor. Day in and day out, week in and week out, I looked in the newspapers and wrote letters with the hope that my work wouldn't be wasted; that at the very end I would see results. At the same time I turned to landsmen whose addresses I had (and asked that) if they hear something new, even rumors about Sislevitcher survivors, they would let me know.

At the end of 1945 there came to me a landsman and friend, Menachim Finkelstein, and he brought with him a printed page in Hebrew published by the Volkovisker landsmen in Eretz Israel, which his nephew had sent to him. In that page somebody witnessed Jews who survived the Nazi camps in Volkovisk . He had 2 names of Svislicher Jews in the list, Neome Levin and Alte Shevelevech who survived; but where they are right now the man didn't know. He had heard a rumor that they went back to Poland. In that same news page it's also mentioned that a Dr. Moshe Einhorn of New York is now in Israel. I also found the address of the Secretary of the Volkovisker Lansmen in Israel, Shlomo Barishkovsky. I wrote right away a letter to him asking about the two Sislivitcher Jews and asked him to find out more details. He answered me "that more than what is in the newspapers, they don't know. Nothing else." But, maybe when Dr. Einhorn will come back he will tell me more about it.

[Page 145]

At the same time I was still reading with thirst the lists of the surviving Jewish people in the Yiddish papers. Once I found lists in the "Foreword" of many Grodno landsmen. The list was sent to the newspaper by the Jewish Labor Committee. I found between the names Berl Lom, with a notice that he had a brother in America. The American Nathan Lom I knew very well because he was my wife's cousin. I also had his address. He lived in New Orleans. I sent right away an airmail letter to Nathan Lom and advised him that he should turn to the Jewish Labor Committee for more information. Also at the same time I wrote a letter through the "JOINT" to Berl Lom in Munich. I told him who I am and where I came from, and asked if he knew anything about my wife's sister who was in Grodno.

The time flew and it was already after Sukkot. I learned that Dr. Einhorn came back already from Israel and that the Volkovisker Lansmen were calling a meeting in the building of the "Forward" to listen to a report about everything which Dr. Einhorn had heard and found out in Eretz Israel. I asked Avramle Kaufman, the Secretary of our Sislevitcher's Society to invite all of our landsmen to listen to Dr. Einhorn's report. But his report was not more than in the previous mentioned pages.

The year 1945 went out and 1946 came in, and there was no more news about the Svislicher Jews. I wrote letters to the landsmen in Israel and also in American and Canada and I thought maybe God will have mercy, maybe I will receive some news from somewhere. And I did.

In the beginning of March, 1946, I received a letter from Eretz Israel. From a lady, Chana Epstein, who wrote to me that she received my address from the Secretary of the Volkovisk landsman, Karlin, and her cousin Riva Laya, who is the daughter of Chaim Shlomo, the religious teacher. From home I knew her family and her Aunt Chana Karlin who lived in Brooklyn very well. I wrote to her and she begged me to help her find her relatives in America. Her mother's name was Chvolkaa, and her maiden name was Slopok. She is searching in America for her mother's sister, Chana. Right after I received that letter Chana

[Page 146]

Karlin with her husband who were also Sislovitchers came to me. The letter from her niece I gave them to read. I then gave them her address in Israel and begged them to write immediately. She did do that. With this, the first work for Chana Epstein was finished.

On the second day I received a letter from Munich from Neome Levin. He wrote to me that he received my address from Berl Lom, that he is a Sislivitcher, and who his parents were. He begs me to find his mother's sister who came from Koseva by Slonim. I knew that in America and Canada there are landsmen who would know about his relatives. I received his letter from Germany at 8:00 in the morning and at 1:00 at night I received an answer from my relatives Cayla and Hershel Zakute in Montreal. They let me know that they had already sent 8 letters from Montreal to landsmen in America and Canada. Three days later I knew where to find Maryasha Panter, a cousin of Neome Levin (Feivle and his wife are cousins). I wrote to Feivle that he should come to me and he came right away. I knew him when he was still a little boy. Now I saw for myself he was a grown-up intelligent person, who had graduated as a radio engineer from McGill University in Canada and here in America he works for the American Broadcasting Company. He took Neome Levin's address and promised me he would do everything he could. He gave me also the names and addresses of Neome Levin's relatives on his father's side who were all in America.

Now I had another problem of how to send over to Neome Levin the addresses of his relatives. The American Post (mail) didn't take any airmail to Germany and to write to him through Jewish Institutions would take too long. So I found a way out of it. I turned to an American family who had a son in the American Army in Germany. I asked them to write a letter to their son, to give him regards from me, and the address of Feivle Panter. That way Neome Levin received indirect regards from me with the address of his cousin here in America. I asked him also to write to me often and I would do everything possible for him. I

[Page 147]

still had to find out his aunt's address in America. And I managed that also. The New York Jewish Newspapers, especially the "Forwards" had long lists of missing relatives. They also carried clips of letter which survivors write to their friends and organizations in America. I want also to note that in the work to find Jewish survivors, relatives and friends in America, a lot of the help was done by Jewish soldiers in the American army in Europe. That is to give credit to the American young boys in the army and the amount of time and effort, and sometimes money, by their going to the D.P. Camps, talking to the survivors and getting additional information and sending it to America. That is the way I received regards from survivors in different camps.

Now we shall return to Neome Levin. I summarized it and sent it to the Yiddish Newspaper, the "Forward" and the "Tog" and there they were published. In that way his mother's sister in Chicago saw the notice and replied right away, giving her Naomi's address.

Now another problem arrived, and I needed to write a lot of letters. Every day more, and I sent them by airmail. A letter like this to Eurpoe would cost $.25, and a letter to Israel $.70, and I had no money for such big expenses. At that time I had already been sick for 11 years. My economic situation was very bad. A family of 4 and we had to live on $90 a month. My children were still young. The older one was 16 (years) and in high school. The younger one was 14 years (old) and still in public school. Even though they were young, when they returned from school they went to work and brought home a few dollars. They were brought up well and every cent which they made they brought home. At that time, in 1946 and right after the war, when the inflation was high, it was hard to get by on $90 a month with a family of four. Rent and electricity would cost $40 a month. Thanks to the savings and efficiency of my wife we were able to get through on a small budget.

But I could not afford a few dollars a week for airmail correspondence. Chana Epstein from Israel asked me why I send with regular mail and not airmail. What could I tell her, that I

[Page 148]

didn't have money for airmail? She would have probably looked at me like I am lazy. In the rich United States a man has to worry about sending with airmail ? But how is that Jewish expression, "God sent the medicine, the healing before the plague." Thanks to my work for the YIVO I had a chance to come in contact with a lot of landsmen to gather material for the YIVO. Once by Lansman Menachim Finkelstein I brought a guest to my house from Montreal, Canada. He was Abraham Cohen, who had a nickname Avremel Kotchkeyer. I knew him already from my childhood. He spent a few hours with me. When he said good-by he took $5 and told me "I want to have a part of your work" I refused to take the money and explained to him that from some people I will never accept money. He went back to Montreal and sent me a letter with the $5 and explained to me that I have no right to deny him a part of this work.

Some weeks later I received a letter from my relatives in Montreal, Kayla and Hershel Zakuta with a money order for $40, with an explanation that it was from some friends that had gathered together in their home. I knew all of them from the old home and they collected the sum to help in the work of connecting survivors in Europe with family in America. I decided that I will accept money from an organized group. So I had already $40 and I could afford with that money to send more airmail than before.

In time more survivors appeared. I found out that connecting them with family in America is not enough; that we had to help them get material goods. In that way I started to organize a relief society for the landsmen from our town. As soon as I came to that idea I wrote a letter to Jacob Elkin. He was the chairman of the "Friends of Sislevitch" and likewise to the secretary, Avramel Kaufman, and his father, Yosif Kappelush. They came to me and we all decided to call a meeting of the "Friends of Sislevitch." The meeting was called for Sunday, May 19, 1946. Only 10 landsmen showed up for the meeting. Many didn't receive the invitation on time because the girl who was supposed to put the invitations in the mail box didn't.

[Page 149]

A committee was picked after the meeting and they came to me . They handed me $131, and gave me the authority to use the money for survivors in Germany as I saw fit. I sent, right away, six food packages to our survivors in Poland , Italy, Eritz Israel, and Russia. Because the survivors didn't stay in one place for long three packages were lost.

Now I started to think about how can we look up more lansmen in America. I used the "Forwards." I used to write summaries in the newspapers of letters from the survivors. I sent it to a co-worker in the newspaper, I. Metsker, who used to print (them) in his Friday's column in the public news page. To the end of the letter I used to add that "whoever wants more information should contact me and I will give them the home address. After this I received a lot of letters with questions from many lansmen. Some letter writers remembered me from home, others asked me who I am. I will give you here an example. I received a letter from a little town, Wilkes Barre, Pennsylvania. The man asked me who I am and what I know about his family in Sislevitch. It was signed by a man, Philip Miller, but he forgot to tell me who he was. I looked around at the letter, I turned it upside down and around. He had on a business card the printed address of a jewelry business . I figured out that if he has a jewelry store he was probably a watch maker in the old home. I started to search my memory of Sislevitch watch makers. Who of them could have changed his name to Philip? I remembered that the watchmaker Alter Kurtze, a boy, his step-brother used to learn that trade and his name was Fivel. New! Fivel must be Philip. I wrote to him right away with these words: "You asked me who I am and you don't write me who you are. So, new! I find that out myself who you are. Your name was Fivel the son of Deborah Sokolniker. I have the information for you about your step-brother Alter Burde. I wrote to him what I know about his relative. The next Sunday he came to my home. I told him again what I know about his step-brother. When he left he told me to tell him whenever there is a meeting of the Svislicher landsmen.

[Page 150]

A second time I received a letter from Minneapolis. The letter let me know that there are a whole group of Sislevitch landsmen (in Minneapolis) who would like to get more information about their hometown. It was signed by a Mr. Mayer. In our town there was nobody with the family name of Mayer. I answered him right away by airmail that he should write to me who he is and give me the name of this town's landsmen. He answered me in a humorous way that he, himself, is not from Sislevitch, but his wife was. He gave me the names of the landsmen in Minneapolis and finished it by a humorous note that "for the work I do I probably get paid with a Shabbos blessing.

A third letter like that I received from Chicago. It was signed with the name Bogan. I didn't know who he was. But I knew that in Chicago there were many landsmen. I sent him a list with the names of all the survivors for which I had an address and told him who of the survivors wanted more information. I also wrote to him that if any of the landsmen wanted more information to write directly to me. At the end I asked him who he is. He answered me that at home his name was Bogomilsky, and that I knew his family from home. This is the way I always received connections with a lot of landsmen in different cities in America and Canada.

I started to think about organizing groups of our landsmen in the big cities in America and Canada. In that way I didn't have to write to individuals separately about similar matters. Besides that about private things. For example when you have to tell someone about their Yartzeit, or when a general thing happens in the history of Sislevitch. In cases like that I would like to write to the leaders of the group and save myself a lot of work. I succeeded in that. The first group was created in Montreal Canada. The activists were Kayla and Hershel Zakuta, Yosif Ain, Avramel Cohen, Jack Gersho, Maryasha Panter, and Mosha Lewis, mine old good friend from the "Bund" in the old hometown. Mosha Lewis (Svishka and Moshka Haskells) had a prominent place in Jewish social life in Montreal. He was the Secretary of the Jewish Labor Committee in Canada. The second group was organized in Detroit. The active people in that group were Riva

[Page 151]

Laya Grodman (Chaim Shlomo, the religious teacher's daughter) and Lowell Liss, Isaac Hershal, the butcher's son.

Later on this group became, and remains, the most active group around. They used to, and still have regular meetings. They still send regular packages to needy Sislevitcher people in the land of Israel, Poland and Russia. They also contributed a lot to the general relief fund in New York which was under the leadership of Jacob and Braha Elkin, Rev. Joseph Kapulish, his son Avramal Kaufman, and also myself, the writer of these lines.

In New York, Hayman Mus was also active. He was not from Sislevitch, but his wife Rifka comes from there, and she is the daughter of Jacob and Bracha Elkin. Hayman is a very educated man and has a rabbinical degree from Yeshiva

University. He also has a diploma from college as a lawyer. He used to help us out a lot with the meetings.

Also in Chicago was an association of Sislevitchers. Rifka Olaynik, Lillian Cohen (Laya Alexanderofsky) and her brother Lev, and Feivel the Goralnik's son, were all active in that society.

Summer passed and it was close to the month of Heshvan when the Nazis killed all the Sislevitcher Jews. That happened on the 22nd day of Heshvan in 1942. I decided to use the Yartzeit to wake up the conscience of our landsmen.

I prepared a system of circular letters to all of our landsmen all over the world so they would observe the Yartzeit.

I did not have an official office with the relief effort. I invited to my house the President, Jacob Elkin, the Secretary Avramel Kaufman, and also Yosif Kapolish, blessed be his memory.

I showed them the system of the letters and suggested they print that letter with 500 copies and add the date of the meeting, and the address of the hall. They would bring back to me the printed circular and I would send them around to all landsmen.

They did everything I asked them to do.

I sent away all the invitations to all the landsmen. I also sent packages of the circulars, forty to fifty per package, to the groups in Montreal, Detroit, and Chicago, and asked them to hold a yartzeit meeting in their town. I also sent them reports of

[Page 152]

everything we had done for the survivors of our hometown and a report of the New York meeting. In addition I have written in general about the destruction of our hometown and attached copies of the letters from survivors so they would have something to read for the meeting, and in that way make people interested in its history.

I did plan everything for them in every detail.

Elkin and Kaufman rented a big hall in the building of the Forwards.

The meeting was on a Sunday, and I don't remember the date anymore. The Friday before the meeting I announced in the Yiddish Newspapers the meeting and they did it for free. The announcement called on all the landsmen to come and give an hour to the martyrs of our town.

Sunday morning before the meeting Avramel Kaufman came to me and we worked out the plan. I gave him the written report of the relief work for the survivors and also some of their letters to read before the meeting.

Because of my illness I didn't go to the meeting. Only my wife went. I sat at home and waited for the results.

And my hopes were realized.

The meeting was a risk. The hall was overflowing with people. The landsmen came not only from New York, but from the whole metropolitan area, Mass., Conn., New Jersey, and many other states, and we collected over $900. The money was not as important as conscience and sentiments of the landsmen being awakened. At that meeting landsmen met each other that had not met for decades. Memories of the olden times of the town were awakened. People were laughing, crying, and hugging and kissing each other. Prominent people were also at the meeting and included the last rabbi from our little town, Rav Yosif Rosen, blessed be his memory. He was the Rabbi of Passaic, New Jersey, and made the eulogy for our martyrs. The Reverend Yosif Kapolish, blessed be his memory, a cantor, said the Yizkor, and everybody cried bitterly. After the Yizkor he repeated with the whole crowd the Kaddish for those killed.

[Page 153]

At the end of the meeting they picked official officers: Jacob Elkin, President, Avramel Kaufman, Secretary, and they elected me Secretary-Treasurer for Relief. They picked also an executive Committee. After the meeting, the whole committee came to my home. They gave me a detailed report of the meeting. They decided to put the money in a bank and they authorized me to use my judgment in helping the survivors with that money.

I received reports of the Yartzeit Committee Meetings from our groups in other towns. In Montreal the group printed my letter and added the date and place of the meeting. The meeting also had good attendance and collected money. Right after the meeting they sent me $100, and a second time $500. In Detroit they collected money and sent me $100 a few times. In Chicago they had a memorial meeting and I received money for the relief effort.

Now that we have money for the relief effort I started to organize a plan to make the best use of the money. Their letters made it clear that they are especially in need of 3 things: 1) food, 2) clothes, and 3) contact with their relatives all over the world.

Previously I have written about contact with relatives.

When it came to food packages I wouldn't rely only on myself. So I turned for advice to my friend Jacob Pat the Executive Secretary for the Jewish Labor Committee, and to the Society of the Russian Jews in New York. They gave me some direction, and I did a little bit according to myself.

The results were quite good. The packages sent arrived at the right addresses and the survivors were very happy. To Europe and Israel I sent the packages through CARE, to Russia through the Society of the Russian Jews or with shipping companies recommended by them.

I didn't have a hard job with the food packages. I sent to the companies checks with the addresses of the survivors and they made up the packages.

But what could I do about sending clothes? We had to pack them and take them to the post office or to the shipping companies. Because of my sickness I couldn't do anything so I turned to my landsman in Detroit….maybe they could do this. The

[Page 154]

answer was a positive one. They took on the whole job. They would collect clothes and money to send them to the survivors whose address I had given them. Here was proof of the loyalty and devotion of the small group from Detroit under the leadership of their President Riva Laya Grodman, the daughter of Chaim Shlomo, the teacher. They worked like bees. The collected the best clothes, and gave away their best things. Everyone opened their closets for Riva Laya and they gave her everything she asked for. We also needed money for sending the packages. A package to Russia, for example, we paid not only postage but also a tax to the Russian Government. The ladies started up card parties or dinners and that's the way they made money to send the clothes packages. The whole effort went like a song (smoothly).

The President, Jacob Elkin, the Secretary Avramel Kaufman, and the Reverend Joseph Kaufman came to me very often to find out about new survivors who had contacted me. We used to help each other think about what else we could do to help survivors.

Once Jacob Elkin and his wife Bracha came to me and asked me to put a telephone in my home. I told them I could not afford one, so they told me it would be a Relief Effort expense. I categorically said NO because I would never allow myself use of money collected for survivors. Then the Elkins promised that they, themselves, will pay for the telephone. They said, "We need the telephone; it's not for you. It is for the work. We want to know all the time how the work goes." So I had no way to argue.

Jacob Elkin was a friend of mine since boyhood. I also knew his wife from home. Here in America they had become very well off. They installed a new phone in my home. The telephone bill was always sent to their place of business.

Later on it proved to be that the Elkins were very right. The telephone was a big addition and saved a lot of work. Instead of writing and waiting for an answer for 3 days, I could get information in 5 minutes.

The Elkins still came to my house often as guests. At one time they told me that I should get paid for my relief work. I categorically denied this and explained that as long as I had no

[Page 155]

money to give, I gave my work, and they gave the money. They told me, "No, your work is worth a lot more than money." So I said "eventually I will get paid." So they asked, "Who is going to pay you, the Shabbos blessing?" They looked at me and Jacob Elkin said "Making fun of me?" I answered him that I am not making fun of anything and explained to him that it says in the Shabbos Blessing (Mee Shabayrew): "Everybody who is active in the needs of society honestly, God should bless him and pay him." They smiled at me and never talked about it again.

The work in 1947 was more lucky. I found more survivors. We needed more work to find their relatives and connect them, one to the other. We need to write more letters, etc., etc.

One side of the wall where I did my work became a wall of tears as they found out their loved ones were lost. On the other side their loved ones were found alive.

My home had a lot of visitors. People use to come from all walks of life. Rabbis used to come, doctors, lawyers. Every Sislevitcher Landsman or ladies who went through New York never left without visiting me.

For our survivors who are spread over many countries, Russia, Poland, Germany, Italy, England and Eretz Israel, the Sislevitcher Support Society was like a beam of light, which shined on their road until they came to places where they settled.

I used to write to them the friendliest and heartiest letters. I used to comfort them, give them courage, calm them down, so that their troubles would soon end. They will still tell all the stories in happy times. A lot of them still keep my letters and I watch over them as a baby.

Quite a few of them are still in contact with me until today. I am already 5 years in the Jewish sanatorium for chronically sick people. I have quite a few visitors from England, Israel, and many towns in America and Canada.

As you will see in my second chapter I prepare to write, if I have enough strength to dictate to my neighbor, the patient, if he will stay long enough to write. I cannot write by myself anymore. My fingers are too weak to hold a pen in my hand.

Additional articles from the Wolkovisker Yizkor Book
(Vawkavysk, Belarus)

[Pages 600-606]

Svislucz
(Svislach, Belarus)

53°02' 24°06'

By Abraham Ain, New York

Secretary of the Svisluczer Relief of New York

The town of *Svislucz*, which the Jews called *Sislevich* or *Shislevich* was already in existence in the 15th century. At that time, it was the property of the noble family of Fokush. In the 17th century, it was transferred to the Krishpionov nobles. In the 18th century, Svislucz became the property of the Grafs Tyszkiewicz.[1] Graf Winzenty (Vincent) Tyszkiewicz contributed a great deal of energy to enlarge and beautify the town. He created a market square which was built up on all sides with houses. He erected a *four story stone building* in the middle of the marketplace, which was about twelve feet square at its base, and about fifty feet high. On the top of the building a formidable metal ball was placed, from which a metallic rod protruded for about three feet. In town, it was said that the building with the metal rod served as a lightning rod, in order to prevent fires started by lightning strikes.

Five principal streets emanated from the marketplace. Two to the east, one to the west, and one to the north and one to the south. Upon entering the town, every principal street had a stone arch on which heavy gates were hung. At night, the gates were locked. Entry to the town was only by way of the principal streets, through the arches. And at night, when the gates of the archways were locked, it was not possible to ride into or out of town.[2]

On the east side of the market, on a stretch of land two blocks long between the Amstibover and Rudavker Gasse, Graf Tishkevich had storefronts constructed, built out of large stones. He instituted market fairs, that took place several times a year. Each of the fairs lasted about four weeks. People would come to these fairs from all over Lithuania, and also from the Polish kingdom. The merchants would store their goods in the stone-walled stores.

Tishkevich planted a town park on the west side of the town, in which there were paths cut out for taking a promenade. On the southwest side of the town, he built a gymnasium that later also became a Teachers' Seminary. Elementary school teachers for the entire Grodno province would come out of there. The Jewish Schulhof was gradually built up over time on the northwest side of town. On the southeast side of town, a number of smaller streets were constructed which were called â€˜the entrenchments.

Svislucz burned down several times. A large part of the town was consumed by fire on three separate occasions. *One time* – In the 1830's; *A second time* – in the 1880's; in the summer of 1910, a large part of Svislucz was consumed by fire. Specifically because of the frequent fires, Svislucz kept on re-building itself, and as a result, its exterior appearance was quite nice. It had many new houses and buildings, among which were two-story structures.

Translator's footnotes:

1. I have taken the historical facts from a dissertation that was written at the Svisluczer Teachers' Seminary by a student named Vaclav Kozlowski.
2. In my time, there were only three archways remaining; the other two, belonging to the *Kerisker Gasse* and *Grodno Gasse* no longer existed.

The Jewish Community in Svislucz

The Marketplace in Svislucz

154

The Community of Swislocz, Grodno District

The exact time when Jews first settled in Svislucz is not known. However, one can be certain that the Jewish community in Svislucz existed there for centuries. It was possible to deduce this from the old Jewish cemetery in the town. The oldest gravestones in the old cemetery, on which the writing was still legible, show dates from the 18th century, but there were older gravestones, whose inscriptions were no longer legible because of their age. In addition to this, there was part of a cemetery where the gravestones and the graves themselves were sunken, and it was barely recognizable that a cemetery had existed on that spot.

By the signs found in the Jewish cemetery, the Jewish settlement in Svislucz was originally a very small one. The settlement began to grow during the 18th century, when Svislucz passed into the hands of the Tishkevich Grafs, and when Graf Vincent Tishkevich built up the storefronts, and instituted the market fairs. The commerce generated by those fairs attracted merchants, who indeed, in that time settled in Svislucz. This marks the arrival of my family, the *Eins*, who came from Grodno, but settled in Svislucz in the 18th century. They were given the additional name, *novikehs*, from the Russian word, *novy*, meaning 'new,' because they were seen as newcomers.

The Jewish settlement in Svislucz grew over a long period of time. According to the census of 1847, there were 997 Jewish souls in Svislucz, and in the following fifty years, the Jewish population there doubled. According to the Russian census of 1897, the Jewish population consisted of 2,086 souls.[1] The population of Svislucz continued to grow. This is notwithstanding the fact, that at that time emigration to England, America and Argentina had already begun.[2] The economic development of the Jewish population was caused by this growth in the Jewish population, and the growth of the Christian population in Svislucz as well.

The Economic Life of the Jews in Svislucz

Svislucz Fire-fighters in the year 1917

Right to left, bottom row (The first four people): Shmuel Maisel, Berel Leib Kapitan, Berel David Ein, Isaac Mottel Uryonovsky; (the first two on the left): Menachem Finkelstein and Alter Burdeh

During the initial years of the Jewish settlement in Svislucz, the Jews occupied themselves in dealing with forest products, commerce in grain, running stores and labor. When Graf Tishkevich built the stores and instituted the large fairs, the incomes from commerce grew. Clubs, inns and taverns were added. In the 1830's, when the stores burned down, there was nobody who would reconstruct them. The Grafs Tishkevich were involved in the Polish uprising and later had to flee the country. Because the stores burned down, the great fairs were stopped, and many Jews lost their livelihood. They began to look for other ways to make a living. A number of them took to trades, especially to tanning leather. Prior to this, a crude form of leather tanning was used to create what was called '*yokhet*' from animal hides. Later on, they began to work with horse hides and finer leather, such as Spiegel (Hamburger), Shagrin and Flat. German master craftsmen were brought in who taught the trade of how to produce a finer grade of leather. The pioneers in the production of finer grades of leather were *Pinchas Bereznitsky, Sender Mintz, Elyeh Rubin* and *his children*, and *Itcheh Pinchas Levinchik*. Leather production grew gradually. Towards the end of the 19th century, the leather industry in

Svislucz consisted of tens of factories and tanneries, that employed several hundred workers. The income of these workers was a great deal more, in many instances two or three times the wages or ordinary workers. Because of the increase in leather production, Svislucz had need for more workers, and many young people from the surrounding towns and villages were brought in there to work in the leather factories. This also expanded the Jewish population of Svislucz. Because of the higher wages of the tanners, their standard of living was higher as well. They ate well and clothed themselves well. This, in turn, provided a good living to storekeepers and other workers. Among the larger storekeepers of that day were numbered: *Zdanovich, Iliensky, Khaliuta* and *Liss*, whose stores were on the same level as an American Department Store, in miniature. In these stores, one could purchase everything from a needle on up to a nickel samovar, a herring, and a good portion of sardines or sprats, a pair of galoshes and a good hat, sweaters, and warm underwear.

In the year 1906, when the new Siedlce-Balagoya railroad was completed, with a station in Svislucz, a mere 3 versts from the town, communication with the larger cities, such as Volkovysk, Bialystok and even Warsaw, was significantly improved. This attracted new people to the town, and the Jewish population continued to rise. Before the First World War, there were approximately 3,500 Jews in Svislucz. During the First World War, when the Germans occupied Svislucz, the Jewish population increased even more, with a number of families that the Germans brought there from the town of Luftch in the Minsk Province, who at that time had remained homeless. The larger number of these subsequently remained in Svislucz permanently.

Economic Conditions After the First World War

After the First World War, the leather factories in Svislucz operated at a low level. The market for finished leather in Russia from Svislucz was completely cut off, and because of this, a large portion of the Jewish population of Svislucz remained without a source of income. Because of the economic decline and the intensification of Polish anti-Semitism, emigration from Svislucz increased. People emigrated anywhere it was possible to go, to Argentina, North America, and after America instituted quotas on new immigrants, a strong emigration began to go to the Holy Land. Despite this, due to natural growth, the Jewish population in Svislucz did not diminish. And when the Nazis occupied Svislucz in 1941, there was a population there of about 3,500 Jewish souls.

In the past several decades, large centers were formed out of the Jews of Svislucz who emigrated from their home town, in the United States, England, Canada, Argentina, and Israel. The largest centers of Jews from Svislucz are found in Liverpool (England), New York, and Montreal. The large majority of the Jews from Svislucz are well established in their new homes, where they are involved in industry, a variety of professions, as well as in community work. It is appropriate to mention two people from Svislucz here, whose names are recognized on a national level. They are *Rabbi Dr. Samuel Belkin* and *David Lewis*. Rabbi Dr. Samuel Belkin is a son of Shlomo Belkin, who was a Hebrew teacher in Svislucz. *Shlomo Belkin* was an enlightened Jew, a good Hebraist, and a contributor to Hebrew newspapers and journals. He was also active in the Zionist movement in Svislucz. Rabbi Dr. Belkin was educated in the Yeshiva in the old country. He received his doctorate in America. He is today the President of Yeshiva College, named for Rabbi Isaac Elchanan, in New York. *David Lewis* is the son of Moshe Lewis,(known in the old country as Moshe Losh, or Moshe'keh Khatzkel's). Moshe Lewis was a member of the leadership of the Bundist movement in Svislucz. He was active in the community and cultural life of the town. Today, he lives in Montreal, where he is very active in community life, and occupies the position of Secretary-General of the Jewish Labor Committee in Montreal, Canada. David Lewis came to Montreal as a young boy. He is a graduate of two colleges, McGill University in Montreal and Oxford University in England. David Lewis could have made a great career for himself as a lawyer. Rather, he chose to follow in his father's footsteps. As a socialist, he gives his time and energy to the SSP – the Labor Party of Canada, where he occupies the position of Secretary-General. His name is well-known among socialist circles in the United States, and among the leaders of the English Labor Party.

Translator's footnotes:

1. The figures for the number of Jews in 1847 and 1897 are taken from the Jewish Encyclopedia.
2. A number of Jewish families in the last decade of the 19th century, emigrated to Argentina, where they settled as colonists in Baron DeHirsch colonies.

[Pages 607-613]

The Destruction of Svislucz

By Abraham Ain, New York

Compiled from letters and recollections that I received from *Simcha Kaplan, Emanuel Goldberg, Meir Galperin, Abraham Stupachevsky, Berel Orlovsky*, and from two Svislucz Christians who were witnesses to the tragedy, as well as *Yerakhmiel Lifschitz* – a partisan who was in Svislucz for several weeks in the year 1946, and spoke with many Christian residents of Svislucz – and from *Nioma Levin*.

In *September 1939*, when the Nazis attacked Poland, the Jews of Svislucz had their first taste of war. German planed bombed a military transport at the Svislucz railroad station. A large number of Polish soldiers were killed there. It didn't take long before Svislucz was occupied by the Russian army. When the Russian army occupied Svislucz, the Polish police commandant and two Polish policemen were shot.

A town committee was established. The local leather factories went over to the Russian regime. A manager was sent that directed the work of these factories. The regime requisitioned the better houses, in which its relocated appointees took up residence. The houses of the *Rabbi, Leizer Khaliuta* and *Meinkus* were requisitioned along with others. Religious education of the children was immediately forbidden, and all the *Heders* were closed. However, slowly, circumstances began to settle down and the populace began to accustom itself to the new Soviet order.

In June 1941, when the Germans attacked Russia, they showered the entire area with leaflets from airplanes, that said they were coming to liberate the entire world from the Jews, and that Jewish assets would be turned over to Christians. Many people elected to flee into Russia, but the way to the east was at that point already cut off.

Svislucz Under the Nazis

Svislucz was captured by the Nazis on *June 26, 1941*. On the first day of the occupation, the German commander issued an order that al the Jews of Svislucz and surroundings should register themselves immediately, and that each Jew should put a white armband on their left arm. A few days later, a new order was issued, which ordered each Jew to put on a yellow patch , ten centimeters wide – one on the front left side of the breast, and one on the rear, right side of the back.

Many young Jewish people were shot on that day, based on informers telling that they were communists. Jews were forced to walk in the streets in order that they not come in contact with the murderers. The Nazis levied burdensome demands for money, gold and also furs. These 'contributions' had to be satisfied in a matter of several hours time. For not complying with these orders on time, many times people were shot on the spot.

The Christian population cooperated with the Nazis to a considerable extent. Many of them took over Jewish houses and stores. Many Christians became converted into ardent followers of Hitler, who bathed themselves in Jewish tears and Jewish blood.

The German commander ordered that a *Judenrat* be established in Svislucz, that should consist of seven people. The spokesman for the *Judenrat* was *Schlachter*, the director of the Hebrew school (he was someone who had moved to Svislucz). His assistant and deputy was *Ephraim Zdanovich*. The other members were: *Mendel Vigonsky, Alter Brudeh*, and *Motkeh Kalmanovich*. The secretaries were: *Dr. B. Meisel*, and *Pin'iyeh Kleinerman*. All the orders from the German authority were conveyed to the *Judenrat*, which was held responsible for carrying them out.

In *July 1941* a *ghetto* was established in Svislucz at the order of the German command, and all Jews were ordered to move into the quarters of their overcrowded ghetto, which consisted of the area from the Schulhof and the *Grodno Gasse*. On the same day that the Jews were supposed to move into the ghetto, it was demanded of them that they bring all their horses and cattle to the marketplace, and turn them over to the Christians.

Life in the ghetto was a real Hell. The enraged German murderers would fall upon the small Jewish ghetto, raining murderous blows on the Jews, robbing them of anything that they pleased. During the time that the Jews lived in the ghetto, they were forced to perform the hardest and dirtiest labor, under the constant eye of the Nazi gendarmes. The Nazis even posted proclamations that Christians were forbidden, under penalty of death, to sell anything to the Jews, especially bread and foodstuffs. Despite this, an illegal trade developed between the Jews and the Christian populace.

In the *Spring of 1942*, the commandant, *Odenbach* called the head of the *Judenrat* to him, and ordered the assembly of all Jews between the ages of fifteen and sixty, men and women, for work on the road that the Nazis were then building between Bialystok and Baranovich. The order had to be carried out immediately. The populace began to pack up, and they went off to do the work. The Jews of Svislucz worked on the road near the village of *Kvatereh*. They did hard labor for twelve hours a day, and did not receive adequate food. Nevertheless, the Jews worked speedily, believing that in this way they would buy themselves out of being killed. But this did not satisfy the Germans. An hour did not go by that the Nazis didn't beat the workers about the head with rubber truncheons. When the Jews could no longer withstand the frightful beatings, they would send messengers to the *Judenrat* in Svislucz to go an plead on their behalf. The secretaries of the *Judenrat* would then come to the workplace, and appeal to the overseer on behalf of the welfare of the Jews. The *Judenrat* also would invite the commandant and other high officials to their homes, and attempt to buy them off with the best articles, the best boots, coats and gold. Each and every one turned over their last possessions in order to ease the plight of the Jews at their hard labor. The Nazis would take everything. A few days would then go by quietly, and they no longer beat the Jews. However, a short time after that, circumstances reverted to the prior situation – in order to extract more money and possessions from the unfortunate Jews. In order to extract even more from the Jews, they took to the Jews with even more brutality. It was in this fashion that the Jews of Svislucz endured through the summer of 1942. At the end of *October 1942* the work on the road came to an end, and the Jews were sent back to Svislucz.

All these tribulations and exertions made life miserable. Many Jews wished for death.

On *Saturday, October 30, 1942* the Christians of Svislucz received an order to provide five hundred wagons for November 1. It became immediately known that these wagons would be used to take away the Jewish population of Svislucz.

The Last Night in Svislucz

On the nights of the *1st and 2nd of November 1942*, Svislucz was surrounded by the German military and local gendarmes – Ukrainians, Poles, and White Russians. On Monday, November 2, 1942 (22 Heshvan 5702), at 5AM, they began to drive the Jews out of their homes. The old, the young, the sick – everyone was compelled to go to the marketplace. Each person was permitted to take along a small pack of personal belongings. These packs were carried on the back, leaving home and gathering at the horse market, in the former stores between the Amstibover and Rudavker Gasse. The marketplace was bounded by a stone wall. At the order of the Nazis, the Christians of Svislucz and surrounding villages gathered there at 7AM, to watch the scene of what was becoming of the Jews. The commandant *Odenbach* arrived at 8AM along with other German officers, and they began to sort the Jews. The young and middle-aged separately, the old and sick separately, and women and children separately. The young and the middle-aged were formed into rows of four abreast, and through the Brisker Gasse, were led off to the railroad station of Svislucz. A large number of the Jews were exhausted, and could not carry their packs, so they took them off their backs and discarded them, freeing themselves from that burden. The Christians, standing by and watching, snatched up these packs. A train transport stood at the ready at the

Svislucz train station. The Jews were packed into the train cars, eighty people to a car. The train pulled away in the direction of Volkovysk. Many, because of a lack of space in the train cars, remained outside. The Nazis rounded them up together, and took them to the nearby *Vishnick Forest*, and they were all shot.

The *older men* and the *women* with *small children* were also taken to the Vishnick Forest through the Rudavker and Hofisher Gasse. Those who could not walk, were loaded onto wagons. Among the Jews taken to the Vishnick Forest were the Rabbi of Svislucz, *Rabbi Chaim Yaakov Mushinsky*, his *wife*, and many of the finest balebatim of the town.

In the forest, large pits had been dug out and made ready. The Jews were ordered to take off their clothes to their underwear. They were lined up in rows of ten, led to the pits, and shot there. According to the telling of *Simcha Kaplan*, the Rabbi gave a sermon in order to soothe the people in their last moments, before they were shot.[1]

The small children were not shot. They were thrown into the pit alive, or their skulls were smashed with wooden clubs before they were thrown in. A Christian writes about this in Russian: "Dyeti Uvyali Derevianemi Kalatushkami." A group of young Jews pulled the convulsed and trembling bodies of the Jews to the pits. These young people were promised that their lives would be spared for doing this work. Nevertheless, they were shot on the following morning. The forest was surrounded by German soldiers, armed with machine guns, in order to prevent anyone from escaping. A few young people though, managed to escape.

The executions continued for an entire day. Towards nightfall, when the murderers saw that they were not yet done with all the Jews, they stood all the people in rows and shot them. It was in this fashion that many who were only lightly wounded came to be thrown alive into the pits that were the graves of their brethren. When the murderers were finished with their handiwork, they went off to the palace in the forest, and indulged themselves in a celebration that lasted the entire night. The group of young people that had assisted in burying their home town brethren were locked up in the cellar of the palace. They were all shot on the morrow. According to the account of *Abraham Stupachevsky*, a number of Jews had the good fortune to escape from the palace. But instead of fleeing to the forests of *Bielovez*, they fled in the direction of the Berestovitz railroad station. There, they were caught and shot.

The possessions of the Jewish populace was gathered up by the Germans and taken to a large grain silo. The better things and furniture were sent back to Germany, the lesser things were sold off or given away by the Nazis, a little at a time, to their local allies and believers in Hitler.

The transport with the Jews of Svislucz arrived in Volkovysk, and there they were driven in to block of six bunkers that had been made ready for them.

The fate of the Jews of Svislucz who were taken to Volkovysk, was no better than that of the Jews of Volkovysk and its environs. They remained in the Volkovysk camp for only a matter of several weeks, where they suffered from hunger, cold, surviving dysentery and outbreaks of typhus, and all the other tribulations that were the hallmark of the day-to-day life in a German concentration camp. Together with the other Jews, they were then sent in transports to Treblinka and Auschwitz, where they were gassed and cremated.

* * *

Only four people survived out of the approximately three thousand Jews that lived in Svislucz when the Nazis occupied the town: *Meir Galperin* fled to Bialystok and was sent to a slave labor camp from there; *Berel Orlovsky* escaped from the bunkers in Volkovysk and joined the partisans; â€˜Nioma Levin lived through the camps at Auschwitz and Dachau and was liberated by the American Army; and *Yerakhmiel Lifschitz*, who went off to Bialystok, and from there joined the partisans. One young girl, *Alteh Shevelevich*, the daughter of Yoss'l Shevelevich (nickname is Yoss'l Brushkeh), also survived Auschwitz. Shortly after being liberated, she was strongly moved to return to her home in Svislucz, where she hoped to find some remnant of her family. En route, she was killed by Polish brigands. They killed her solely because they saw that she was a Jewish girl.

In addition to the four surviving Jews from Svislucz previously mentioned,, there are, to date, 38 additional Jews from Svislucz. A number of them had lived in other towns, others fled the camps, and hid themselves in the forests and fought the enemy as partisans, and most of these are among those who served in the Red Army or were sent to Siberia.

No Jews live today in Svislucz anymore. The few who turned to go back there after the liberation of the town, took one look at the desecrated [Jewish] cemetery in which the town takes pride, left immediately to find a new home.

* * *

I have written this article in memory of the Jewish martyrs of Svislucz, among whom were my two sisters and their families, who were shot in the Vishnick Forest, gassed and incinerated in the crematoria of Treblinka and Auschwitz.

Let the lines of my article serve as memorial markers that cover the scattered and dispersed graves of our brethren and the ashes of the Svislucz Jewish martyrs, who were taken from us in so tragic a manner.

Let us honor their memory!

Translator's footnote:

1. Simcha Kaplan was not in the Vishnik Forest. What the Rabbi had spoken about, he heard from Christians when he came to Svislucz in 1946. Simcha Kaplan served as an officer (captain) in the Russian-Polish Army.

NAME INDEX

The Community of Swislocz, Grodno District

www.ingramcontent.com/pod-product-compliance
Lightning Source LLC
Chambersburg PA
CBHW050404110426
42812CB00006BA/1795